Praise for

When Crisis Strikes

"Chronic stress ranks among the most serious threats to human health and longevity. And surprisingly, its pivotal role as it relates to degrading our most coveted health assets is generally underrecognized. But whether brought on by sexual abuse, dealing with an alcoholic parent, having a child with special needs, or the seemingly ever-present threat of serious viral illness, chronic stress can be recognized, contextualized, and ultimately ameliorated. And this is the mission of *When Crisis Strikes*. Drs.Love and Hovik eloquently lay bare how chronic stress insinuates itself into every aspect of our lives and provide the tools to relinquish ourselves from its influence. Especially now, this book is essential."

—David Perlmutter, MD, #1 *New York Times* **bestselling author of** *Grain Brain and Brain Wash*

"*When Crisis Strikes* is an indispensable book that will guide you through the inevitable crises we will each face in life. While the circumstances of your brain in crisis will be unique to you and your situation, Drs. Love and Hovik will show you the science of your stress response, the impact on your mind and body, and practical steps to feel better and come through it stronger."

—Mark Hyman, MD, #1 *New York Times* **bestselling author**

"Artfully weaving the biology and psychology of human crisis (a.k.a. stress), Drs. Love and Hovik educate us about what is happening in our minds and bodies, and empower us to master it. We all have faced some alarming crisis or another—it is part of life. How we identify it, command it, and recover from it is critical to our mental and physical health. This book offers invaluable guidance. Really, any book that teaches us to give our crisis the finger is worth a read."

—Reuben Sutter, MD, founder and medical director, Sage Neuroscience Center

"Charming, poignant, and profound. In the midst of the unprecedented global crisis that the COVID pandemic is, readers will find the book full of deep insights and practical advice."
    —**Elkhonon Goldberg, PhD, director, Luria Neuroscience Institute, and clinical professor of neurology, NYU Grossman School of Medicine**

"Drs. Love and Hovik have written a scientifically sound book that is also informed by clinical experience. This book is well written and humorous, and it shares many relevant examples of how to use their 5-step model to recover from various kinds of life crises."
    —**Per Normann Andersen, PhD, professor, Inland Norway University of Applied Sciences**

"Approachably irreverent, yet always sincere, Drs. Love and Hovik have packed their book with practical, science-based advice for dealing with stress. Following the steps laid out in *When Crisis Strikes* will improve both your life and your experience of it."
    —**Jonathan Betlinski, MD, director and clinical associate professor, Division of Public Psychiatry, OHSU**

When Crisis Strikes

5 Steps to Heal Your Brain, Body, and Life from Chronic Stress

Jennifer Love, MD

and

Kjell Tore Hovik, PsyD, PhD

Foreword by Daniel Amen, MD

CITADEL PRESS
Kensington Publishing Corp.
www.kensingtonbooks.com

ISBN-13: 978-0-8065-4081-8
ISBN-10: 0-8065-4081-8

First Citadel trade paperback printing: January 2021

10 9 8 7 6 5 4 3 2 1

Printed in the United States of America

Electronic edition:

ISBN-13: 978-0-8065-4082-5 (e-book)
ISBN-10: 0-8065-4082-6 (e-book)

Dedicated to—

*My mom—the woman who first demonstrated to
me how to thrive amid multiple chronic life crises.*

*My besties, who have been lighthouses
guiding me to shore through countless storms.*

*My patients, who allow me the sacred privilege of helping
them explore (and sometimes excavate) their minds.*

—JENNIFER LOVE

––––––––––

*To the untapped potential in each of us
to shine and change the world for the better,
one friend at a time.*

—KJELL TORE HOVIK

Contents

Foreword

Daniel G. Amen, MD,
Founder and CEO of Amen Clinics

EVER SINCE I BECAME A psychiatrist nearly forty years ago, I have been helping people in times of crisis. Yet until now, there has not been such an accessible book with a clear road map on how to navigate crises from a brain-health perspective so as to help you avoid chronic stress and prevent the sympathetic nervous system from getting stuck. This is why I am so excited to write the foreword to *When Crisis Strikes: 5 Steps to Heal Your Brain, Body, and Life from Chronic Stress* by my friend and longtime Amen Clinics psychiatrist Jennifer Love, MD, and her Norwegian colleague, neuropsychologist Kjell Tore Hovik, PsyD, PhD.

Dr. Love is one of my most trusted physicians and helps see some of our most complex patients. In addition to psychiatry, Dr. Love is board certified in both Addiction Psychiatry and Addiction Medicine, which means she has seen hundreds of patients and their families in deep crisis. I've known her to calm down patients who have brought drug-induced violence into her office. She has sat in tears and in long silences with mothers and loved ones of patients lost to drugs, suicide, and tragic accidents. She walks through life with people who are slowly declining from multiple sclerosis, traumatic brain injury, cancer. She knows how to compassionately help people who feel electrocuted by trauma. Dr. Hovik, alongside his research efforts, has spent most of his professional career working clinically with the most serious life crises imaginable, those involving thought and brain disorders that make you see things, hear things, feel things, say things, and do things that nobody with a healthy brain would ever consider. From patients without any insight into the impact their behavior has on their family and society to patients who are so despondent about their lives that they self-harm and try repeatedly to end their lives, he has given these individuals and their families hope and a path out of their mental quagmire. His neuropsychology training helps him treat struggling patients of all ages from a biological, psychological, and social perspective, understanding how all of these factors have shaped each individual and provide clues to their recovery process.

With their long training and experience treating the most serious brain disorders, these superior professionals have written an accessible and essential guidebook for anyone caught in a harrowing life situation. With the five-step model they have developed, they help you discover how your brain works with your body's natural stress response system; how environmental and emotional cues can cause physical reactions like muscle tension, pain, lowered sex drive, and apathy; and how you can achieve balance and harmony in your life by committing to the five-step process.

As I write this foreword, the world is in the middle of the worst pandemic in recent history, with widespread stay-at-home orders, worldwide death, fear of dying, mass layoffs, and damage to the global economy—all mixed with the killing of George Floyd by four Minneapolis police officers and the subsequent outrage, protest, and societal unrest. We are in effect in the midst of a cluster of pandemics: COVID-19, the fight for social justice, and the ensuing mental health pandemic of anxiety, depression, posttraumatic stress disorder, addictions, domestic abuse, and divorce.

To understand this mental health response, we need to look at how the brain and body react in times of extreme stress. When crisis strikes, our emergency alarm system, the stress response, activates the sympathetic nervous system and prepares us either to put up a fight or flee a dangerous situation. The fight-or-flight response causes rapid physical changes, such as increased heart rate, shallow breathing, a rise in blood pressure, slowed digestion, muscle tension, immune system shutdown, and more. Without effective crisis management strategies, stress can become chronic, causing your sympathetic nervous system to get stuck in either the "on" or the "off" mode. When it is stuck on, you are trapped on high alert and are more likely to suffer from anxiety, panic attacks, headaches, muscle tension, digestive issues, and immune system issues. When it gets stuck in the off position, you feel fatigued, depressed, have brain fog, and have trouble with attention and focus.

Many lives have already been upended by the stacked stresses, and mine was no different. The day the world stopped for me was March 10, 2020. My new book, *The End of Mental Illness*, had just been released and I had been traveling to promote it. I was scheduled to film the *Mel Robbins Show* in New York City the next day when I got a call from the producer saying I shouldn't come because their studios were being shut down. I was sad, but also glad not to get on a metal tube (plane) with the coronavirus. A few days later both my parents (ages ninety and eighty-eight) spiked fevers and tested positive for COVID-19, and were rushed to the emergency room at our local hospital. Fortunately, they shared the same hospital room, but I couldn't visit them even though I was in charge of supervising their medical care.

But the crisis was just getting started. One of the young employees in our Manhattan clinic was sick with the virus and ended up on a ventilator for five weeks. The first week, we all wondered if she would pull through. We had to close our New York clinic for three weeks and all of us were on edge with the uncertainty. All eight of our Amen Clinics were in coronavirus hot spots. My parents were both discharged five days after they were admitted to the hospital. My mother recovered quickly, but my father had little energy and a persistent cough. I was getting ready to take him to the doctor on May 5th when I got a frantic call from my mother saying my dad was not breathing. Despite the paramedics' best efforts, that day my father became an angel.

Despite my forty years' experience helping patients work through life crises, every crisis is uniquely personal. I had found myself thrust into multiple crises involving dear family members, employees, and society all at the same time. Because of my long training, I was able to isolate the stress-inducing threats and manage the situation while continuing to take care of my family, friends, employees, patients, and myself at the same time. Even though my crises were very personal to my life and situation, my underlying stress response and managing it involved the universal principles described in this book. *When Crisis Strikes* is the guide anyone facing a serious emotional upheaval can use to identify and calm the unique set of stress-inducing variables besieging them. I wish I had this book forty years ago; I am glad we have it now.

Drs. Love and Hovik offer a straightforward five-step process to manage any life crisis. These rational steps lead to what Martin Seligman, PhD, the father of positive psychology, calls "posttraumatic growth." This is when a crisis can lead to a greater appreciation of life; a changed sense of priorities; warmer, more intimate relationships; greater sense of personal strength; and recognition of new possibilities or paths for one's life and spiritual development.

This book is full of practical ideas and it also shows their application with powerful case studies helpfully grouped under the topics loss, trauma, family crisis, chronic illness, and existential crisis.

At some point in life, pandemic or not, we all experience crises that make us cry or bring us to our emotional knees. Now is the time to learn how to deal with them effectively to avoid any lasting physical or emotional damage and to promote posttraumatic growth. This engaging, practical, user-friendly guide will help you do it. The Five Steps have helped people suffering from the worst life crises imaginable; they can help you too. Lean in.

Preface

Jennifer

I T'S TUESDAY, AND I'M SITTING on a conference call with my literary agent and a Norwegian. I can't discern which feels more foreign to me, the agent and the foreigner or the realization this project is going to catapult me from my safe and comfortable medical practice (my introvert's dream cocoon) into the public. I've been encouraged by conference attendees, patients, and a few colleagues to do this for years, and when I met Kjell,* I was easily convinced not to fly solo on this project. He says things that make me stop and think the way few people can. I think you'll like that about him, too.

I tend to be formal and methodical (I brominated hydrocarbons in a chemistry lab before going to medical school, so yes,

---

* Think *Shell*, like a seashell, but place a *T* in front and sneak in a *C* somewhere in the middle—*Tschell*—or just call him *K-jello*, but don't tell him it was my idea.

I'm a science nerd), and I like wrapping things up neatly in packages with bows: here you go, understand *this*. Kjell's thought processes, on the other hand, are as far-reaching, omnidirectional, and limitless as the mass of curls atop his head. I am intuitive and emotionally sensitive, and Kjell can burst through a door and address a problem with grand force, confidence, and direction. (Interestingly, he thinks the reverse is true, but until I see his evidence, I'm sticking to my theory.) Together, I figure, we can speak to everyone.

Writing with a coauthor has its challenges, especially considering the stubbornness—I mean *strength of opinion*—we each bring to the construction of these pages, but the beauty is that in life (and in a life crisis) humans are a blend of personality traits; those of us who are quiet will sometimes need to be loud and fierce, and those who are extroverted and larger than life will sometimes need to be mindful and soft.

In the early stages of writing the proposal for this book, when Kjell and I were wondering whether anyone would even be interested in reading it, someone in the publishing industry offered a bit of encouragement. "Everyone," he said, "will go through at least one or two of these crises in life. Everyone needs this book." All I could think was, *One or two in life? Is this guy insane?* Here's my 2016: In February, I met a kind, interesting person, and we started dating. Three months later, I met with a geneticist and a surgical oncologist at Stanford Hospital who both recommended I undergo radical surgery to prevent or lower my chances of getting a highly deadly cancer that runs in my family. I believe the exact words were, "Do this five years ago." The nice new boyfriend couldn't fathom why I was so distressed, and we ended the relationship. So, alone, I got second through eighth opinions (I know a lot of good doctors), and all the doctors gave the same advice. I selected a surgical oncologist, had my life-altering surgery, and a few days later developed a postoperative complication and almost died. This brings us to Thanksgiving 2016, when I was finally out of the weeds and could start moving forward. So, within a nine-month span, I started a relationship, had horrible medical news, endured a breakup, navigated massive life-changing decisions alone, had some pretty important pieces of my body yanked out by a surgeon, started a medical protocol, and nearly died. I'm pretty sure that's like five or six crises in one year. *Do not get me started on my life.* So yes, in retrospect, I suppose I have to agree my early concerns about the universality of the topic of "life crisis" were possibly unfounded. If you've had a year like my 2016, this book is for you.

Kjell Tore

Yes, Jennifer and I are a bit different. If traveling through life is like a long drive, where you start out on a wide-open, multilane freeway like they have in sunny Southern California and then transition in time over to a single-lane icy country road like we have in Norway in winter, both of us are on that rather slippery section of road at this point in our lives. In the back seat of her car, Jennifer has the book *Kitchen Confidential* by Anthony Bourdain and a takeaway tray of sushi, while I have three kids arguing about what is the best ski wax for cross-country skiing in minus 10 degrees Celsius (14 degrees Fahrenheit). And while Jennifer is driving a German car with heated seats and studded tires (for solid grip on icy surfaces), I'm driving a British sports car (couldn't afford an Italian one) with an awesome sound system and all-season tires. I prefer to slide and accelerate around the icy bends; Jennifer doesn't.

Despite the differences in packaging, however, when the moose jumps out from the forest and stands smack in the middle of the road, our instincts are pretty much the same: slam on the brakes! From then on, however, our intellectual styles betray contrasting educational and clinical training. As a medical doctor, Jennifer tends to think from the inside out: "What effect will crashing into the moose have on my blood pressure, and how will that influence my thinking and emotions?" As a psychologist, I tend to think from the outside in: "What motivated the moose to jump out into the road, is there a calf close behind it, and how should I react if I just killed his or her mother?" Then insights from my PhD in neuroscience kick in, and I think about how to regulate my thoughts and feelings to deal with the crisis effectively. Despite different angles of approach, it turns out Jennifer and I reach the same conclusion: five basic steps will help us survive the crash with the moose or any other heart-stopping event.

Jennifer is the kind of medical doctor who takes time with her patients. An appointment with her starts precisely on the hour and actually lasts an entire hour. She wants to make sure that you are on the right path to health and that you understand what you need to do to stay on that path. Experiencing her genuine conscientiousness of spirit and force of intellect when discussing patient cases is what attracted me to collaborating with her.

The original model I suggested for the Five Steps was in the form of a hand with five fingers (based on the idea that the hand had been described as the "outer brain" by a philosopher I admired in my youth).* Jennifer had to think about the idea for a few days, but came around to liking it—just as long as we didn't call it "the hand model." By the way, Jennifer has long, slender fingers, while I have chubby, Viking fists. Despite our inner and

---

* In his book *Kantian Imperatives and Phenomenology's Original Forces*, Randolph C. Wheeler writes about Immanuel Kant referring to the hand as the human's "outer brain." Cultural Heritage and Contemporary Change, Series I, Culture and Values, Volume 3, 2008.

outer differences, though, we are both passionate about communicating practical mental health strategies to those in need.

While life crises are unavoidable, we hope the tools we will share with you in these pages can help you avoid the crippling effects that chronic stress can have on your brain, your body, and your life in the weeks and months ahead, and perhaps even turn your life into the success story you deserve.

When Crisis Strikes

Introduction

═══════

Jennifer

Y OU ARE UNDER A GREAT deal of stress. I know this, not because I have the gift of telepathy or prophetical insight—that I know of, anyway—but because you're reading my intro, and people who are carefree, who ride their unicorns from Los Angeles to Fiji every other Wednesday *just because they can* don't read intros for books like this. Something has happened to you or someone you love and you are overwhelmed by emotions: anxiety, grief, indecision, uncertainty, anger, helplessness, hopelessness. Whatever your unique circumstances, one thing is sure: you are drowning and in need of a lifeline. If you've read the preface, you know that I've needed one before, too.

So what's going on in your life? What are you feeling? Why do you feel this way? Asking *why* is my favorite thing to do. So naturally, when patients come into my office in a life crisis (possibly similar to the one you're experiencing now), I want to know all of the physical and emotional symptoms they're

experiencing so we can address the crisis wisely and compre-
hensively. When a patient comes into my office with a
symptom, before rushing to alleviate it, I always ask myself *why*
the symptom is there. One of my pet peeves is hearing about
people who go to a doctor, complain about a symptom, and are
immediately handed a prescription without any discussion. For
example, someone will go in to discuss problems focusing his
or her attention and leave with a prescription for a stimulant
medication for ADHD after ten minutes. Many of these people
invariably end up in my office, having tried numerous medications for poor focus, to no avail. Why? Well, the doctor never
asked that question. There are many reasons someone may
have poor focus; ADHD is just one of them. In my office, I treat
poor focus as a symptom rather than a diagnosis. Anxiety is
one of the more common causes I see, and I've diagnosed more
than my fair share of thyroid disorders, hormone abnormalities,
and substance use disorders. A stimulant won't treat any of
those issues.

So the first thing I always do is ask *why*. Then I start every
treatment plan with an explanation of what I think is going on
so my patients and I are on the same page. So, why are you
stressed to the point of crisis?

Stress is apparently *expected*, as humans come prewired to
manage it straight out of the womb. We have an intricate stress-
response system built into our brains and organs, and at the
time of birth, our stress-response system expects to respond to
stress the way our lungs expect to respond to air. We are hardwired for it.

Well, kind of. We are hardwired for survival, like when early
humans had to escape wolves and bears while gathering berries.
The "fight-or-flight" response is meant to save our lives in acute
emergencies. But there is a limit to how much stress the system
can handle.

So what happens when stress is chronic? When multiple stressors pile up at once? When multiple *chronic* stressors pile up? This is where it gets interesting (or infuriating, depending on whether I'm wearing my scientist hat or my human hat). Our brains release a cascade of chemicals, which in turn cause various organs to release more chemicals, resulting in a wide range of physiological changes that can leave us exhausted, unproductive, fat, sick, impotent, and perusing a book on life crisis. In other words, you can't sleep, can't have sex, can't accomplish what you want and need to do, and now you have a muffin top or a panda belly, or maybe an extra jowl.

Awesome.

When you are in the throes of a life crisis, it's helpful to understand all the strange changes going on in your body, so I'll start us off in "The Science of Stress" chapter with an explanation of how the human stress-response system is wired. I'll explain why you may be staring at the ceiling at three o'clock in the morning, why you've had a cold for four months straight, why you're suddenly allergic to everything, why you can't zip up your jeans, why you started clenching your jaw, and why you feel you're crawling out of your skin.

Kjell and I will then tag-team throughout the book, first introducing you to a five-step model that will help you work through any life crisis. Then we're going to apply the steps to real life crises—losses such as divorce, financial ruin, and betrayal, and medical illnesses such as cancer, chronic back pain, and depression. We'll apply the steps to family crises such as addiction, raising a child with special needs, and having a partner or parent with a chronic illness. We'll address traumatic experiences such as bullying, growing up with an alcoholic parent, abuse, and a mass shooting. We will even address spiritual and existential crises such as the heartbreak surrounding suicide or losing one's sense of purpose or meaning in life.

Our goal is for this book to provide you with:

- An understanding of your physical symptoms
- Practical steps to solve your current life crisis
- Experience seeing the steps applied to various situations.

Then we'll circle back to the beginning and outline a program of lifestyle interventions that you can use to battle the physical symptoms caused by your life crisis: the fatigue, the insomnia, the muffin top, the feeling your finger is plugged into a light socket—all of it.

Your brain is in a crisis. Let's recover together.

PART ONE

Stress and the Five Steps

The Science of Stress
(a.k.a. Why You Feel Like Crap)

Jennifer

S CIENCE MAY BE A SWEAR word in your vocabulary, but I promise this is worth it. When we're in a chronic crisis, oftentimes our bodies seem to fall apart, and it's helpful to have a basic understanding of why this happens so that you can make the changes necessary to feel better.

I was going to start this chapter with a clever vignette about my patient Eddie (not his real name). I was organizing my thoughts about the myriad of symptoms associated with the brain's crisis-response system when I was struck by a realization: I likely spent close to fifteen years of my life in adrenal stress. *Why am I reading a book by a doctor who didn't even know how to diagnose herself for fifteen years?* you may be wondering. In my own defense, I am actually excellent at self-diagnosis and, like every other current or former medical student, an overachiever in this arena. (Med students are notorious for thinking they—or their classmates—have every disease they study that week, including completely ridiculous ones like phytobezoar* or psychiatric ones like histrionic personality disorder.) However, the neurotic tendencies of my colleagues (and my own) will be put aside for the time being. Back to why I'm not a horrible doctor: the diagnosis of adrenal stress doesn't actually exist. While the body's system for handling stress was taught in medical school, there was simply no explanation as to how chronic stress effects the system, and to be honest, there is so much information thrown at med students in just four years, I only noticed its absence in retrospect. I have experienced multiple life crises over the years, but this one spans about a decade and a half. I'll call its story "My Crisis Saga" for a bit of nostalgic, med student dramatic effect.

My Crisis Saga

When I was younger, my life's fuel was more stress than joy, but I was too busy to notice. I started college as a nursing major, switched to a joint major in biology and chemistry after two years, and graduated three years later with honors and an extraneous fifty to sixty credits. While earning top grades, I was cajoled (read: forced) into working as a lab assistant, a supplemental instructor for biology and chemistry courses, a research associate for professors in the departments of chemistry and

---

* A *phytobezoar* is one of millions of unnecessarily complicated terms for med students to learn, which is typically seen under the rarest of circumstances: over-ingestion of persimmons, which, in large quantities, are so fibrous the stomach can't process and pass the contents, which then sit inside the stomach, like a hairball in a cat's stomach, causing nausea, vomiting, decreased appetite, and feeling full after eating small amounts of food. *Trichobezoar*, in case you're now wondering, is the medical term for "hairball." And yes, humans can get them, too.

microbiology, and a tutor and a grader—jobs that paid under minimum wage and took a considerable amount of time, but were done in pursuit of the much-coveted glowing letters of recommendation required for medical school. As you might guess, I slept about four hours a night. During my third year of college, my mom was diagnosed with what was supposed to be a terminal cancer. Her oncology team at Stanford Hospital described her recovery as "miraculous," but for an only child with a single parent, the weight of almost losing the sole person who had ever supported and loved me unconditionally weighed heavily on my heart.

By the time medical school began, I was running hard on perfectionism and adrenaline. I was thrilled and intimidated by the opportunities ahead, sinking under the weight of anatomy and pathology textbooks, trying to squeeze in intramural basketball games and dates, and occasionally vacuuming my seriously crappy apartment.

Despite my exhaustion, I could never sleep well and never once woke feeling rested. I was constantly hungry. I lived on coffee and diet soda. I had a breast lump scare, mononucleosis, and severe joint and muscle pain, developed an autoimmune thyroid disorder, and endured five or six sinus infections *every* winter. I started "taking call," which meant once or twice a week I had a thirty-six-hour shift in addition to my regular clinical duties. It was not unusual to work nearly a hundred hours a week in the hospital and clinic, without counting the hours of study required to pass rigorous examinations.

My specialty and subspecialty training took another five years. I continued to work between eighty and a hundred hours weekly, and the stakes became much higher: a mistake could harm or even kill someone, and the appropriate hypervigilance combined with my underlying perfectionist tendencies only exacerbated my stress.

I was elected president of the department's resident organization, which meant I led weekly meetings of resident gripe sessions and was tasked with putting out the fires of personality clashes while serving as an intermediary between disgruntled residents and mostly disinterested faculty. I was asked to serve as one of the chief residents during my fourth year, which meant I had to write lectures and teach in addition to my other duties. I worked overnight shifts in the emergency department, served on a citywide suicide prevention task force, spoke at conferences, helped a colleague open a clinic for pregnant drug users, and when the state legislation held back our funding, participated in a letter-writing campaign to get the funds released. I had so little time off, the idea of wearing pajamas became a luxury, as was being at home, and I morphed into a person whose only hobbies involved things that can be done at home in one's pajamas (mostly baking and watching *Top Chef* or *Ice Road Truckers*, if you're wondering).

One day, I folded my arms and felt rolls where my ribs were supposed to be. I knew I had been gradually gaining weight over the years; hospital food is hardly healthy, and at two in the morning the only place in the hospital to get food is the coffee cart, and the only food at the coffee cart is brownies, so I kind of knew it was in the cards. I refused to step on the scale, but I knew my clothes weren't fitting, I was always tired, and this former athlete could barely get through a thirty-minute workout.

What happened to me—to my body—during all of those stressful circumstances spanning about fifteen years? *My brain's crisis system went completely bonkers.* I slept poorly, craved sugar, and suffered from irritability, fatigue, and burnout. Does this sound familiar? I bet you've struggled with similar symptoms. You're stressed, stretched, internally preoccupied, and have lost your grasp, your edge, and your mojo. You might be in such an enormous crisis you think you'd rather trade your life crisis saga for mine! So now that we're all bonded in misery, let me explain *why* this happens to us, so we can move on and do something about it already.

The Body's Stress-Response System

There are two types of people in the world: those who love science and those who don't feel the need to discuss whether the USS *Enterprise* could *actually* travel to another galaxy through a black hole in order to enjoy a film series. While the latter some-what perplex me, my college science professors discovered I was gifted with the ability to communicate with this majority group, the disinterested-in-science students, and I was coaxed into being a sort of translator, breaking down science into easy-to-understand concepts for my classmates.

As we examine the science of stress, I'm going to use two lan-guages: first, a simplified version of the basic science, and then, a translation of sorts using analogies. It doesn't matter which you follow: there's no exam here. Just bear with me, and within a few pages you'll have a basic understanding of the physical origin of your life crisis symptoms.

As humans, we are hardwired to manage stress via an intri-cate feedback loop between the brain and the adrenal glands. Three anatomical structures are the key players composing what is referred to as the *HPA axis*: the *hypothalamus* (in the brain), the *pituitary gland* (also in the brain), and the *adrenal glands* (we have two, one on top of each kidney). Together, these areas maintain *homeostasis*, which is just a fancy scientific term for metabolic balance within the body. In other words, the job of the HPA axis is to create and maintain a relatively stable in-ternal environment, even when we experience physiologic changes. The hypothalamus senses the environment, then sends a chemical message to the pituitary gland, which then sends its own chemical message to the adrenal glands, which respond by releasing several chemicals, with cortisol as the final step in the feedback loop. Once the hypothalamus senses the cortisol, it stops sending its message and the system can stop and rest until the next stress comes along.

Think of it this way: The brain is Command Central, like 9-1-1. When distress is sensed, the hypothalamus assesses the level of danger and calls 9-1-1 right away; the 9-1-1 operator (the pituitary gland) dispatches a message to alert the first responders. The adrenal glands contain the first responders. Once the first responders address the crisis, dispatch is notified, stops coordinating the response to the call, and goes back to waiting for the next call.

The adrenal glands pack a pretty big punch considering their diminutive size. It's wild to realize something the size of an olive has so much power over how we feel. You might think it should be *at least* the size of a Cadbury Creme Egg to serve any purpose, but I don't recommend saying so in medical circles, not that I speak from experience. Each adrenal gland is divided into zones (like a Cadbury Creme Egg, hello . . .), which have different functions. The center (called the medulla) releases epinephrine (a.k.a. adrenaline), which is the main chemical responsible for the fight-or-flight response. So if you're walking along and suddenly encounter a bear, within a second your hypothalamus has sensed the danger and ordered the release of adrenaline, which prepares you to fight or run by redirecting blood away from certain areas (like your bowels) to essential survival areas (like your muscles and brain); it dilates the airways in your lungs to maximize oxygenation, and increases your heart rate and the strength of the heart's contractions. All of this combined gives you the best chance for survival in that moment as you face the bear.

Think of the adrenal medulla as the military response to Command Central's dispatch. It equips your body to fight or evacuate the area—whichever is the best strategy for the given situation.

Surrounding the adrenal medulla is the adrenal cortex, which is divided into three main zones, strangely referred to as "zonas" because half of what we learn in med school is Latin:

- The zona glomerulosa
- The zona fasciculata
- The zona reticularis.

You don't have to remember their names, but think of these three zones as other first-line responders: firefighters, police, and paramedics. Here's what the three zones do:

- The zona glomerulosa secretes a hormone called aldosterone, which regulates sodium and potassium levels (electrolytes) and fluid balance.
- The zona fasciculata secretes cortisol, which helps maintain optimal blood sugar levels for the body's current needs.
- The zona reticularis produces sex hormones, like progesterone, DHEA, estrogen, and testosterone.

Before you get all confused and think your high school biology teacher failed you, estrogen and testosterone *do* primarily come from our ovaries or testes. However, in order to keep balance (there's that word again), the zona reticularis produces small amounts of both sex hormones, which is why both men and women have both estrogen and testosterone, although in vastly different quantities.

So what happens when this system is repetitively stimulated? Or when the system is stimulated in non-life-or-death situations that are emotionally toxic nonetheless? Like getting laid off at work and having to look for a new job or finding out your spouse is in love with someone else? The adrenal glands respond to stress the same way, regardless of the source of the stress. In other words, your adrenals don't understand the difference between a bear attack and a spousal betrayal: stress is stress, and whether it is physical, emotional, psychological, existential, infectious, or environmental, these hormones will be released by your adrenals.

Each component of the HPA axis's feedback loop requires time for recuperation before the next stress comes along, and when the rest doesn't occur, symptoms of adrenal stress can appear. The concept of adrenal stress is somewhat confusing because it isn't technically a recognized medical disorder. We have diagnoses for the state of hypoadrenalism (also known as Addison's disease, which is a rare condition in which the adrenals do not produce adequate amounts of the hormone) and hyperadrenalism (overactive adrenal function, also known as Cushing syndrome), with "normal adrenal function" somewhere in the middle. However, there is no clearly defined diagnosis for someone with adrenal functioning that lies between normal and nonexistent. It is possible to develop symptoms from what is best described as a sluggish hormonal response from the adrenal glands. This is what is often referred to as "adrenal stress" or "adrenal fatigue." Whether or not adrenal stress is an official diagnosis, the physical symptoms of chronic stress make sense when we look closely at adrenal functioning. Keep in mind there is a lot of individual variation in this (which is part of the diagnostic conundrum). Let's look at the process hormone by hormone.

Epinephrine (Adrenaline)

The release of adrenaline causes muscle tension, which prepares us for physical action (running from the bear, for example). What happens when we are stressed by a traffic jam or sitting in a conference room during a meeting with a micro-managing supervisor? Under these conditions, a rush of adrenaline can produce feelings of jitteriness, physical tension, and frustration, especially when getting up and moving around isn't possible. Over time, chronic stress leads to tense and sore muscles, jaw clenching, tight hamstrings, neck and back pain, even headaches. Think about it: if adrenaline is telling our muscles to fight or flee the scene, we are wired to do just that, and just like the HPA axis, our muscles then need to recover before resuming normal functioning. If instead, after being primed for action, our muscles are held in a state of inactivity (sitting behind the wheel of the car or in the conference room), the muscles become tense. With chronic stress comes chronic muscle tension. Let's finally get to Eddie:

On the insistence of his therapist, Eddie begrudgingly came in for a consultation. He gingerly lowered himself onto the couch, wincing, grabbing his back. He assured me he was fine and could handle it. "I can handle everything, actually; it's my therapist who says I should talk to you." He was in therapy to address his alcohol use, and for the past few months, he had experienced fatigue, low mood, sleep disruption, and low sex drive. Our discussion revealed his stress over his mother's cancer, the strain he faced working at the family restaurant, and his inability to start his own business. In addition, he was recently engaged and looking for a house to buy with his fiancée. He had injured his back years ago playing sports, but for some reason it started acting up again, slowing his every move, turning his restaurant shifts into torturous experiences. This self-proclaimed tough guy who could handle anything on his own could barely lower himself onto a couch.

Eddie was in his predicament for a number of reasons. In addition to muscle tension from chronic stress, Eddie was going to great lengths to hide from me and everyone else his high anxiety, and parts of his brain called the basal ganglia (we have two, a left and right) were overactive. The two basal ganglia aren't part of the HPA axis, but they are neighbors of the hypothalamus in the brain. They are associated with multiple brain pathways, notably movement, as well as emotion (feelings of calmness vs. stress or worry). I frequently point out to patients like Eddie the basal ganglia's link between emotional stress and stiff, sore muscles. If you can calm your brain, you can calm your muscles; if you can calm your muscles, you can calm your brain. We'll revisit this in the chapter "From Pain to Sane," when we discuss how to reclaim your brain and body. For now, just remember there are very real brain and body connections resulting in stress-induced body pain.

Aldosterone

If you're a salt craver during a brain crisis, aldosterone (or an imbalance thereof) may be your culprit. During *acute* stress, the release of aldosterone by the adrenal glands causes a quick electrolyte shift, resulting in sodium retention. Sodium retention in this case is actually a good thing because it causes water retention (water follows salt: the more salt you have in your body, the more fluid you retain), which increases blood pressure and blood volume, so our muscles and brains have access to oxygen and nutrients for optimal functioning while we're trying to outrun (and outsmart) a bear. Over time with chronic stress, as the adrenals can't keep up and start to fatigue, the opposite can manifest: the sodium balance shifts and sodium is excreted through the kidneys and water follows, which can lead to salt cravings and lowered blood pressure. Lowered blood pressure commonly leads to dizziness or lightheadedness upon standing.

I don't remember having salt cravings during my brain crisis saga (I was a total carbohydrate/sugar addict), but for years, I experienced light-headedness upon standing, despite my best efforts at staying hydrated. Conventional medicine told me to drink more fluids. If the adrenal stress theory is true, drinking tons of water wouldn't have helped my symptoms of low blood pressure unless I had enough salt intake to enable me to retain the water I was drinking. You can understand why the traditional medical approach doesn't define adrenal stress or fatigue when you realize how symptoms can differ between people. But recognizing your symptoms and understanding their origins will help you decide which of the stress interventions outlined later in the book you'll want to follow.

Cortisol

This is where anyone worried about a muffin top or a fat belly needs to perk up and pay attention, as cortisol seems to be the key player in what I refer to as the "panda bear syndrome" (also not a recognized medical diagnosis, but very, very real). One of cortisol's jobs is making sure the necessary organs have enough fuel to meet their increased energy demands during a crisis. Energy is used by cells in the form of glucose, which produces fast energy. Insulin, released by the pancreas, is what helps glucose get into the cells. When cortisol levels spike during *acute* stress, the fats, proteins, and carbohydrates we've eaten are converted into glucose and delivered into the cells by insulin. We then burn all these calories running from, or fighting with, the bear. With *chronic* stress, the adrenal glands can't keep up with the body's demand for cortisol (they need rest, remember), so cortisol levels start to decrease while the demand for energy in the body remains elevated. (When stress is ongoing, your tissues and cells think you're still running from a bear, so they demand fuel in the form of glucose.) As cortisol levels decrease, however, the conversion of fats, proteins, and carbohydrates to glucose falls, and the body mistakenly thinks it needs glucose, which leads to sugar cravings. This begins a harmful cycle: sugar cravings entice us to drink soda or eat cookies, we get a spike in energy for an hour or so, but our glucose level then plunges, which places further stress on the body and adrenal glands, and this plummeting glucose level (called hypoglycemia, or low blood sugar) drives us to eat sugar again. We gain weight because insulin is increased, the glucose we ingest goes straight into the cells, and the excess is stored as fat. The most common areas for weight gain under these circumstances are around the belly and around the face (what I lovingly refer to as growing jowls).

In addition to controlling glucose balance, cortisol also has anti-inflammatory effects and protects us against the autoimmune process. Perhaps in the past you may have had a serious illness or injury and been prescribed oral or injected steroids to calm inflammation. Such steroids (like prednisone) are related to cortisol. With *chronic* stress, suboptimal cortisol levels can contribute to an *increased* inflammatory response, so you can develop allergic reactions (to environmental allergens or foods) or may be more likely to experience autoimmune issues. This may be why I developed an autoimmune thyroid problem when no such issue runs in my family, chronic sinus infections, and most devastating of all, the onset of respiratory allergy symptoms (unrelenting cough, mucus) after eating cheese (which was always my favorite thing on the planet). As if the crisis isn't enough, now I can't have my go-to comfort food? The universe can be cruel indeed.

In an agonizing double whammy, cortisol can impair sleep both when it is too high (why would you sleep when running from a bear, right?) as well as when it is lowered by chronic

stress. Under normal circumstances, cortisol is released in regular patterns to maintain homeostasis, which contributes to a
healthy sleep-wake cycle, or circadian rhythm. When cortisol
levels are abnormal, sleep onset can be impaired and sleep maintenance can be disrupted by nighttime hypoglycemia. This leads
to difficulty getting up in the morning, daytime fatigue, mood
changes, irritability, and brain fog (caused by both poor sleep
and hypoglycemia, in another of cortisol's double whammies).

Sex Hormones

Ovaries are the primary source of estrogen in women and
testes the primary source of testosterone in men, but the adrenal glands make both estrogen and testosterone in smaller
quantities in both sexes. The decrease in libido seen during
stress may be caused by decreased testosterone production by
the adrenal glands. This actually makes sense. If you need energy
to run from a bear, the body should hardly be distracted by activities geared toward reproduction, right? But over time with
chronic stress, lowered libido can be devastating. Sex is awesome, and losing the desire (or ability) to participate causes
discouragement and frustration and lowers our quality of life.
Because of the sex hormone changes in the adrenal glands, some
women may also experience worsening premenstrual syndrome
(PMS) or exaggerated symptoms of menopause and perimeno-
pause. These changes in our sex hormones affect not only our
own bodies during a crisis, they also affect our partners and/or
our families (via irritability and hormone-based mood swings).

To summarize, during times of acute stress, our bodies are
intricately wired to improve the chance of survival. Why our
bodies aren't better at managing chronic stress is a total mystery.
While it is certainly an interesting topic for medical debate, we
have more pressing needs to address, such as, *How on Earth am*

I going to manage my current life crisis? Later in the book, we'll circle back to discuss how to address sugar and salt cravings, weight gain, muscle pain, and fatigue. But first, let's look at our five-point model of crisis management, and then we can practice applying the steps to real-life situations.

Introduction to
the Five-Step Model

Kjell Tore

A FEW WEEKS BEFORE CHRISTMAS a few years ago, a close friend of mine, Nina, learned that her father had been diagnosed with pancreatic cancer and had about six months left to live. A risky new surgical procedure could possibly extend his life another few months, but nothing was certain. In her forties, Nina was already struggling with her own health, job, and family problems that had pushed her coping reserves to the brink. Through everything, her father had always been a secure anchor in her life. With this latest news, the normally positive and loving mother of two teenage boys felt so overwhelmed that she was left gasping for air. Now she felt like both of her feet were tangled in the chains of an anchor cast overboard, and she was just waiting to be yanked and pulled down into a deep abyss.

It's natural to panic when facing a crisis with threats and arrows incoming from every direction. You feel an urgent need to act, but choosing the right action among a dizzying array of urgencies can be paralyzing.

The devastation Nina felt in her moment of crisis is no different than what most people experience numerous times in the course of a long life, but some are better at coping with "hell raining down" than others. The Five Steps presented in the following chapters are based on what Jennifer and I have found to work in crisis situations—lessons learned from our own experiences and decades guiding patients through horrific upheavals. Even though Jennifer and I have different starting points (doctor of medicine vs. doctor of psychology), working on the front line of extreme mental disorders for years has given us insights into positive change processes.

Here is a quick overview of the main points in the five steps, which we envisioned as representing the five fingers of a hand when we developed the model.

Step One is *Get a Grip (thumb)* which involves gaining an overview of the situation and then naming and examining the *what* and *why* behind the distressing emotional feelings you are experiencing. In short: what is the problem, and what is the meaning of the problem to you personally?

In Step Two, *Pinpoint What You Can Control (pointer finger)*, you identify the issues that need to be addressed to move forward on your way out of the crisis. It involves focusing on the things you can do something about and developing strategies to deal with the things you have no control over. In short: what can you control, what can't you control, and what can you do about the things you can't control?

Step Three is *Push into Motion (middle finger)*. Here you find motivation and opportunity to get down to the business of straightening things out in a concrete manner despite your fragile state. In short: tap into your fighting spirit, give your crisis the middle finger, and get to work. Here we also describe a resource in your brain that you can use to regulate the thoughts, feelings, and behaviors causing havoc in your daily life.

After actively working through the first three steps, Step Four, *Pull Back (ring finger)*, isn't about strength. It is time to reflect on your life, simplify, and balance the fierceness of Step Three with softness. The key message here is to be kind to yourself.

The final step, Step Five, *Hold On and Let Go (pinky finger)*, helps you tap into the precrisis you, but now renewed after having worked through the earlier steps. Holding on to the positive and letting go of the negative both require strength, which the pinky finger, working together with the other fingers of the hand, provides. The sum is greater than the individual elements.

It took days for Nina to overcome the initial shock of the news about her father. The news triggered a cascade of emotions that replayed a torrent of negative future scenarios over and over again in her mind. Our brains are wired to be more sensitive to negative and threatening thoughts than positive and uplifting ones, so when knocked off balance by devastating events or news, a road map and guardrails can be helpful to get your mind back in balance.

Nina's story and that of some twenty other individuals and families struggling with life crises are presented in the next chapters to illustrate how the five steps can help you weather your storm. Each vignette presents a brief description of a character in distress and the context of his or her crisis. Nina and the characters portrayed in the vignettes are not real people, and their stories are not true events. However, they are composites of patients we have worked with over the years, and their circumstances are typical of the stories we've heard in our practices. Some of these scenarios may be similar to what you've experienced in your life. But even if the details are different, the acute cognitive, emotional, and behavioral stress responses they evoke will likely be familiar. It is our hope that we can lead you to a safe haven to weather the storm you are currently walking through and build your resilience for whatever future challenges you may face.

Step One:
Get a Grip

―――――――――

Kjell Tore

T HE MIND'S NATURAL REACTION TO any sudden sight, sound, or distressful event is to focus its full and undivided attention on the threat. And the body will follow. If you ever had an older brother jump out from behind the dumpster while screaming bloody murder late at night when you were taking out the trash, you know what I'm talking about. If the unexpected act is loud and intense enough or if you are sensitive or in a vulnerable state of mind, the mayhem can overwhelm you and initiate a cascade of terrifying thoughts, feelings, and fears. The initial stress response can pass or it can linger. If it lingers, it can paralyze you and have the potential to turn into a chronic condition.

Our automatic response for perceived danger evolved long ago in order to prevent us from becoming some animal's lunch. It was not intended for dealing with complex modern crises such as financial ruin, humiliation, bullying, chronic pain, family upheaval, or an existential meltdown. Certainly the danger of encountering a saber-tooth tiger was more life threatening, but these contemporary crises pose long-lasting threats to our well-being and have a serious impact on our attentional resources. Without the ability to smartly control what thoughts, feelings, and actions to focus on (our attentional resources), we are essentially flying blind—and risking crashing into a mountain of troubles.

Since the brain and body are wired for reacting fast and furiously, our natural response system actually hampers our ability to deal with complex threats. We need to learn how to override this system. Crippling and chronic threats demand a more sophisticated response approach. The good news is that there is a way to gain control over your automatic response system.

Before we can start controlling or regulating anything, however, we need to take power over a key brain function that will open a treasure trove of possibilities: our attentional resources. We need to *get a grip*.

Step One: Get a Grip

Three actions will help you override the brain's automatic tendency to freak out and push the escape button when your brain is at its boiling point.

1. Take control of attentional focus.
2. Answer the question: *What is the problem?*
3. Examine the problem's emotional foundation.

What Is Attentional Focus?

When I refer to attentional focus, I'm not talking about the type of mental focus you have when you knit a loop stich for the millionth time, when you watch a weekly sporting event on TV, when your mom or dad yelled at you as a kid and told you to look at them, or even when you are out driving. All of these examples involve fixing your eyes in a certain direction and diverting a small amount of your brain's attentional capacity to what you are looking at; most of your mind is still full of thoughts and emotions. This type of superficial attentional focus is part of the brain's system of parallel processing, the ability to apply several layers of attentional focus on both conscious and subconscious levels.

The attentional focus you need to Get a Grip is the type that integrates as many attentional levels as possible. Not only what you see, not only what you smell, not only what you hear, not only what you are thinking about doing later in the week, not only the uneasy feeling you woke up with in the morning—all levels!

Think about the first time you read a word, the first time you put together individual letters to evoke an image inside your head that you could see, hear, feel, and/or taste (likely in kindergarten or even earlier). You put together the letters *D*, *O*, and *G*, and your mind filled with an adorable image, that puppy smell, the slobbery wet kiss on your face, and the overjoyed emotion your beloved pet brought to your encounters every afternoon when you came home after school. The amazing achievement of suddenly being able to read also filled you with immense confidence: you were now a "code breaker," and your life had changed forever. Several levels of attentional focus were aligned when you made this discovery. This is the type of attentional focus we want you to have in the Get a Grip process: as many attentional levels of mind, heart, and body aligned here and now that fill your heart with a warm, glowing feeling of joy when you crack the code to solve your crisis.

Many do not remember the first time they ever actually read a word. I don't. But I do remember the first time I read a word in

Norwegian. I was about six years old, sitting on a toy box we had brought from Norway to California, on top of which my mother had glued a bright orange piece of shag carpet. I was sitting right on that itchy shag carpet and wondering why she had put floor carpet on a place to sit. It was a warm day, so in addition to the carpet scratching my skin, it was also making me very warm. At the very same time, I was intensely studying drawings in a Norwegian children's book that I got as a birthday present from relatives back home. I noticed strange letters in the text that aren't in the English alphabet: Æ, Ø, Å. Weird, I thought. Just like the shag carpet prickling my bottom was "weird." I kept looking intensely at the storybook, at the images and lettering. Strange how thoughts and feelings from one attentional train of thought weave back and forth across varying levels of attentional focus. And, by the way, what was that wonderful smell coming downstairs from the kitchen?

The book I was looking at was a collection of traditional Norwegian folktales. My mother used to read to me from this book at bedtime, so I had heard the stories verbally a number of times. But suddenly, I found myself reading the letters and words in the storybook. "Imagine that, I can read Norwegian," I thought to myself while I was at the same time irritated about the hairy shag carpet prickling my behind. I moved over to the other side of the room to continue reading in a more comfortable place, as the shag carpet was pulling attentional capacity away from my interest in finishing the story.

Thoughts of that experience are suffused with sensory memories—the feel of the carpet, the smell of my mother's cooking. It's a clear example of the different levels of attentional focus that can happen in the same instance. Remarkable! But this trait is not so great when we need to really focus in order to learn something new or solve a problem. So the question is, how do we get to that place where our attentional focus is not going in all different directions willy-nilly, if we can't just move our body to another setting?

Think back again to when you first started reading. Think about how you would decode the three symbols *r*, *e*, and *d* (*red*) and how they would bring to mind a favorite crayon, a barn door at your grandparents' farm, a delicious apple, or a huge, noisy vehicle with flashing lights and sirens racing through the city streets. Simple markings on a piece of paper or chalkboard brought to life a universe of images, smells, tastes, sounds, and rhythms inside your heart and mind. Magically, all of these different sights and smells were bound together with a common thread—red. But now imagine that this automatic process grouped different areas of focus together with something that caused you pain and distress. Let's say, for example, you experienced a traumatic accident in which you saw lots of blood and thought you might die. Now, every time you see a red crayon, a red barn door, a red apple, or a red fire truck, your heart and mind might be filled with fearful images—the blood and gore, the fear and dread you felt during the accident.

Changing bad associations requires both effort and intention. You can't be drinking too much, on your phone for hours, or escaping into video games or dramatic love affairs. Getting a grip on your problem requires letting go of escape strategies. It won't be as hard as it sounds, but we need to get you to this fully focused state of integrated attention to start the Get a Grip process.

Stop Escaping and Take Control of Your Attentional Focus

A technique we use with professional athletes to take control of and integrate their attentional focus so they can perform a task optimally is to ask the question, how are you feeling right now? If you take the question seriously, you scan your mind, body, and heart to bring focus to your here-and-now state. It can work like a reset button. Your body, heart, and mind (focus) need to be fully with you for you to function optimally in the present moment. If a golfer can feel the balance in his feet, his grip on his club, his stomach responding to breathing deeply and calmly, his eye muscles relaxed, and shoulders at ease, he is ready to make the putt.

My friend Sigurd, a successful ski jumper, climbed out onto the beam at the top of the K120 hill for the second round of ski jumping at Lysgårdsbakken in Lillehammer. It was the national championships. He was already in the lead after the first round, so he only needed a long second jump to secure a win. In the waiting area before he climbed out onto the beam, the jumper in second place wished him luck and said he hoped that his knee injury had healed (wink, wink). Sigurd hadn't been thinking about his knee injury at all, but now he was! The competitor's comment brought to mind the pain of his knee injury in the last World Cup, when he crash-landed spectacularly at the bottom of the hill at over sixty miles an hour. This distracting thought made him also think about what he would say to the press if he lost his lead because of a catastrophic second jump. All of these distracting thoughts were swirling in his head as he was climbing into position for a jump that needed perfect mind and body synchronization to successfully fly him four hundred feet down the hill.

Luckily, Sigurd recognized what was going on in his mind, so he went into his preset routine to integrate his focus for the task at hand. He started with deep, rhythmic breathing. Then he let unhelpful thoughts wash over him like waves at the beach. His focus became the here and now. He scanned his body, sensed his mind and body coming together to unite with his honed skills to get into his flow zone. This routine was easy for him because he had practiced it a thousand times before. He signaled to his coach he was ready, his coach signaled back that the wind conditions were safe, and he was off for one of the best ski jumps of his career.

You can see how integrating attentional focus can help a person perform at his or her best on a specific task in the moment. Crises can be even more chaotic, with a multitude of thoughts and threats that prevent you from integrating your focus, not to mention irritating distractions like the telephone ringing off the hook as you're trying to finish a make-or-break project, an angry spouse hurling insults at you, or the chaotic noise of a hospital emergency room. So let's look at how integrating your attentional focus can be applied to a crisis situation.

Countless threats and distractions try to steal your attentional resources, but it's possible to regain focus. Just imagine that all the interactions, insults, outbursts, and pain swirling around during your crisis are symbols—letters or words—on a chalkboard or on a canvas. It's up to you to choose to give them meaning or not and to link them together or not. Think of these letters or words as being on the outside of your mind and body, not inside. They can enter but can only stay if they are invited. You decide which ones are invited to come inside and "sit by the fireplace" with you (as we say in Norwegian). The letters invited take on the meaning that you give them. Remember that the space by the fireplace is limited, so as we work through the next steps, only invite one set of letters making up one word or issue at a time. Integrating your attentional focus in this way will help you separate the relevant from the irrelevant and help you gain control over your attentional focus. All the other letters that are not needed for your purpose can wait outside in the cold and cool off (it can be very cold in Norway, so sitting by the fireplace is a big thing here).

Various Traditions of Focusing Attention

The goal of gaining control over your attentional resources and focus is to achieve a state of mind and heart in which growth and positive change can happen. Like when you first learned to read. I refer to this as integrative focused attention.

People in other professions use different terms for basically the same concept. A modern term used by many to describe an integrated state of focused attention is *mindfulness*. Others use the terms *grounding* or *earthing* to indicate a similar state of mind. My religious friends use a term like *faith*. The term *meditation* also refers to an effective way of training the mind's ability to attain an integrative state of focus. If you have experience with any of these focusing traditions, you already have a head start on your Get a Grip process.

Why Focus on a Problem?

When a crisis detonates an explosion of thoughts and emotions in your body, like a meteor landing in a sandy field, putting a name on the cause of the explosion is the only way to discover a solution. It's not that there will be any less dust in the air; it's just that you will have something concrete to focus on so you don't get blinded by the chaos of particles swirling around you. If you are afraid of heights and find yourself standing on the ledge of a tall building, looking down into the abyss is not advisable. A better strategy is to focus on a specific, concrete object close at hand that you can hold on to so you can calm your racing heart and thoughts.

I have a fear of heights, so in situations in which I have to attend a gathering on the sky deck of a skyscraper, I carry a smooth stone in my hand that I can rub or squeeze. It helps me change my attentional focus from the fear of falling to something close, solid, earthy, and soothing.

ATTENTIONAL FOCUS VS. ATTENTIONAL DIVERSION

The fastest route to the immediate relief of a modern-day crisis, one that many opt for, is to dive into attentional distractions like alcohol, pot, pills, junk food, gossiping, the Internet, shopping, work, unhealthy relationships, and other deviously mind-diverting pursuits. All of these activities steal our attentional focus away from the problem at hand. You may think, *Great, a nice break from the awfulness of the situation.* But not so fast. The continuous repetition of these common avoid-and-escape strategies may dull and delay the painful angst of an impending crisis for some time, but your subconscious is still parallel processing feelings of dread about the disaster deep down inside your body and brain. The by-products of all this under-the-radar processing will eventually surface in the form of classic symptoms of psychological distress—sleeplessness, anxiety, depression, body pains, anger, aggression, and irritability. It's unavoidable. And the avoid-and-escape strategies will do nothing to resolve the underlying problems keeping you from moving on to a healthier, happier place.

Let's revisit Nina from the "Introduction to the Five-Step Model" chapter. If you remember, her crisis was triggered by learning that her father had a deadly form of cancer. This information activated a range of emotions similar to what she'd feel if she were standing on a high ledge looking out over an abyss. To make matters worse, the prognosis was that her father had only a few months to live, which would keep her crisis simmering every day for months. What you don't yet know about Nina is that although her father has been her main source of support, he has also been a dominating influence on her life choices. His harsh criticism of her had a crippling effect on her self-confidence and caused her to develop a negative self-image. Instead of rebelling against him in her youth, Nina became increasingly dependent on him. Nina also has her own health problems. Five years ago, she was involved in a terrible car accident that left her hospitalized for weeks and in physical therapy for over a year. She still suffers from limited physical ability and is in constant pain. Her medical issues caused her to miss a lot of work, and her employment situation is now precarious. The icing on the cake is that her husband has become increasingly distant, spending more and more time at the office. She also has two rebellious teenage boys at home, and with her husband hardly ever home, she is carrying much of the parenting on her own. Nina can't attribute all of her problems to her father, but she often tends to blame him for her problems. In a way, that has also been a crutch she has leaned on to avoid taking responsibility for her life.

Nina is overwhelmed by stress, full of despair, and paralyzed by the enormity of her situation. But there is something she can do. Nina needs to name her problem in order to change her focus from a frightening abyss all around to something solid and constructive to work with. We will be using Nina's story in the following chapters to help illustrate the Five Steps.

Nina's crisis is complex, and a technique to help her define her main problems is to write key words, descriptions, and labels about her crisis on pieces of paper and attach them to a bulletin board or even something symbolic like a cutout tree. Even a notebook will do. There is something about the physicality of writing and creating something on the outside to mirror a thought or feeling on the inside that can help her better "see" her problem. Like the smooth stone I use when I am in a high place, having a meaningful object outside your body that you can see and touch helps to slow and calm an unsettled mind and heart. (A teddy bear or a pacifier served a similar function for most of us in the past.) At the very least, the process of writing by hand helps slow down the pace of your thoughts, like taking deep breaths can slow down a racing heart.

After doing this exercise, Nina defines her main problem as the fear and the uncertainty of how she will be able to deal with future problems in her life without her father around. She has always been totally dependent on him. How can she manage after he is gone? She is not simply sad that she is losing him, she also is terrified of losing her crutch in life. It is fear that is fueling her crisis and will intensify her crisis.

Now that she's identified her problem, she needs to understand it. Why is Nina's fear so intense? She needs to look into her past to understand the foundation of the intensity of fear she feels at the prospect of losing her father. Only after she fully examines her problem can she start to address it.

Here's what the strategy looks like:

1. Name the problem.
2. Examine the thinking behind the emotions generated by the problem.
3. Replace it with alternative thinking.

Examining the Emotional Foundations of the Problem

Putting a name or label on the pressing problem is an excellent start to help visualize the problem, but it's just a start. Nina is still up on the ledge, but her resting pulse has slowed because she now has something external to focus her thoughts on. Now she needs to examine why her fear is so distressing.

Nina starts this process by selecting a few emotionally salient issues related to the problem she has named. For each issue, she examines the thinking upholding her feelings of fear. Then she needs to explore how to change her ways of thinking about her fear.

Nina's Fear of Losing Her Father

Nina thinks through the emotional underpinnings of her fear of not being able to deal with problems in the future when her father is gone. The reality of her having several areas of vulnerability in her life (health, job, relationship, kids) that could crash at any moment adds urgency to her fear.

As she thinks through the inevitable loss of her father, she recognizes that her fear is grounded in her belief that she cannot deal with difficult problems by herself. Her fear is that she cannot cope without her father. How did this insecurity develop, and what aspect of her thinking is perpetuating her dependence on him? Could it be her habit of always calling her dad at the first sign of trouble—asking him to fix things for her? She realizes that she never learned to deal with difficult issues on her own in childhood and always avoided dealing with problems later because her father was always there to fix them for her.

Nina comes to realize her habit of asking her father to fix things for her has reinforced her feelings of helplessness when faced with a challenging situation.

Nina's Recurring Downward Spiral of Negative Thoughts

The second issue Nina discovers is her habit of allowing her fears about her inability to solve problems on her own spiral out of control. She recognizes her tendency to focus on negative experiences in her past and to imagine catastrophic consequences in the future. She recognizes this may have to do with her father's harsh criticism about some of her past decisions and her acceptance of his criticism as truth. She thinks back about how her father would always second-guess her choices. Whenever she tried something different, her father would tell her how she should have listened to him because he knew what was best for her.

Nina realizes that her father's focus was always on the choices she made that did not work out and not the choices she made that worked out well. Thinking back, there were plenty of choices she made that worked out well. But she is not used to balancing negative thinking with positive thinking when fear kicks in. She falls into the trap of taking over her father's critical voice, accelerating her fall down into what feels like a bottomless pit.

Nina's Lack of Areas of Mastery

The third issue Nina discovers and chooses to explore is the broader issue of why she is struggling in so many areas of her life and feels so out of control. She has lost any sense of self-confidence, so has no area of success present in her mind to counter her downward emotional spiral.

Nina thinks about how many areas of her life are the way they are because she has just let them happen. Instead of striving for and insisting on her own areas of success to boost her self-confidence and self-esteem, she neglects herself to support others in their goals and lets others decide what is important for her. Perhaps much of this is the result of her father's domineering influence on her in childhood; she did not learn to create her own way, but gave in to his commands and demands. Instead of channeling useful traits from his forceful personality into her own personality, her father's domineering influence crippled her free spirit. She accepted his criticism instead of shutting it out. She developed a conflict-avoidant style, which she now sees robbed her of the drive to find her own areas of mastery.

Nina spends time reflecting over how her conflict-avoidant style is manifested in her interactions with others. She sees this tendency in her relationships with her husband, her children, and her employer. She gives everyone what they want. She subconsciously strives to avoid criticism and conflict at all costs. Other people's priorities become her priorities.

Commit and Follow Through

There is no way to go around a personal crisis: you have to pass through it. It's like the golfer who shanks her tee shot on the first hole into the lake. There's little use in her throwing her driver into the lake or running her golf cart into a tree; it won't even help to stomp off the course and go home. (If she did, imagine the impact on her self-confidence the next time she is on the tee.) And she can pretend all she wants that it didn't happen or make all the creative excuses she can think of for the miss, but the bottom line is that the ball is in the lake and a new ball needs to be put in play for her to move forward. On the golf course, there are simple rules for her to follow to get back in play and through the course.

Life is a bit more complicated than a round of golf, however, and the people on the tee with you in life may not be as understanding and forgiving as those accompanying you on a weekend round of golf. In any event, with the clear steps we provide in this book, you can get through life's worst "shank" with a positive outcome.

I know you are dealing with a difficult situation and it's a lot to handle. I want to reassure you that you will get through your crisis, but mindful work is needed, and you might need to ask for help. A family member, trusted friend, religious leader, or skilled therapist can support you through this process. As a start, if you are able to stop escaping, mobilize your integrative focused attention, name your problem, and think through the emotional underpinnings of central issues relating to your crisis, then you should be able to get through the steps on your own. If you are so stressed or your mind is so fragmented that you are not able to bring the needed level of attentional focus to your crisis, we encourage you to reach out for professional help to aid you through this process. Avoidance strategies are lurking around every corner, and the naturally occurring self-destructive processes at play in times of crisis can be difficult to tame on your own. But whether going it alone or with help, by having started the process of reading through the steps in this book, you are already on a sound path through your storm.

Step Two:
Pinpoint What You Can Control

Jennifer

O NE OF THE WORST FEELINGS for many of us is the sense of losing control. Whether you're about to go under general anesthesia for surgery or you've rested your case and are awaiting the jury's ruling, your situation has drastically changed and you no longer have any input, any control over the next steps your life will take. For most of us, this feeling is unsettling; for some of us (control freaks in particular), it can be terrifying. Whatever life crisis or parade of horrible things has led you to this book, the feeling of helplessness will likely insert itself into your story at some point.

A few years ago, my friend—a California girl to her core—moved to Indiana. We marveled at all of the "firsts" this move would require of her: tornado insurance, a ginormous winter heating bill, and everything that comes with snow, from hats, boots, gloves, and coats to scheduling time for shoveling the driveway every time she leaves the house. What she wasn't prepared for was the first time she hit black ice on a major thoroughfare with her young child in the backseat. She described what it felt like the moment she lost control of her car: the change she felt in her hands as they gripped the steering wheel, the oddness of moving in a diagonal trajectory. Despite her attempts to prepare for hitting ice, nothing prepared her for the shock of instant, unanticipated loss of control, that moment when her son's life was no longer in her hands as she slid across the road toward another car.

For my patient Abe, this instant shock of helplessness arrived in an envelope left under his car's windshield wiper while he was at work. When he picked it up, he felt an oddly shaped object inside. When he opened the envelope, he found a note and his fiancée's gorgeous engagement ring. Eight months prior, he had left his dream job to move with his fiancée across the country so she could attend graduate school. He left his friends, his social and business networks, his neighborhood. The job he found wasn't particularly fulfilling, but he was happy because it paid the bills and would pay for his dream bride's dream wedding. He was so in love he optimistically sacrificed everything to create a life with his partner. He paid the hefty nonrefundable deposit for their wedding venue. He paid for the wedding dress hanging in the hall closet he was forbidden to open. He bought the decorative pillows for their couch, the special pot she wanted for cooking, the floral sheets he didn't really like but she loved, the candlesticks for their table. He created a home with his fiancée. And now, on a Wednesday evening after work, he stood next to his car holding the ring he worked so hard to afford, the ring he went to a dozen shops to find, the ring of his partner's dreams, and a note saying she had left that day and was transferring to another university out of state. In his hand, he held the end of their relationship. There was no fight, no discussion, no warning Abe had seen. In a moment, the life he knew, the life he had curated and cherished with his fiancée, ceased to exist. His hands were on the steering wheel, he was navigating his way peacefully, when suddenly Abe hit black ice. His opinion didn't matter. His love didn't matter. His actions wouldn't matter. Her decision was out of his control, and he found himself suddenly veering in an unanticipated direction.

Scientific (but Interesting, I Promise) Theories About Control

Curiously, control doesn't actually mean the same thing to everyone, but people tend to fall under one of two main worldviews: what we call an external locus of control or an internal locus of control. (Here we go with unnecessary medical Latin again: *locus* means "location." Basically this means, do you believe control of your life resides outside of yourself or within yourself?) It's really more like a personality continuum rather than a strict one or the other, but understanding how you view your problems will help you master Step Two.

Someone with an external locus of control tends to attribute outcomes to external circumstances. Several years ago, a couple I knew became pregnant. They repeatedly announced, "We're in shock. We weren't expecting this at all. This is definitely a miracle!" I happened to know that the wife had stopped her birth control months before and that despite saying they weren't trying, they certainly (based on what she herself told me) weren't doing anything to prevent pregnancy, so each time I heard them tell someone, "It's a miracle!" I wanted to say, "Actually, it's biology!" (I didn't, by the way, because I'm only snarky in private with my best friend, but I really wanted to.) I had known this couple for years. I had heard the way each of them spoke about life events: meeting each other was "fate" (rather than his *deci-*

sion to walk over and talk to her), and not getting a highly competitive promotion was "discrimination" (rather than a result of the *tantrum* she had thrown at work). And despite publicly fighting like two coyotes over the world's last remaining raccoon baby, seemingly at constant war with one another, they said things like "Destiny brought us together" and "Even though marriage is totally miserable, we're sooooo meant to be." For each of them, the ultimate decider of life's events was external.

Someone with an internal locus of control tends to experience a sense of responsibility over outcomes. My neighbor has an incredible garden. She grows avocadoes, lemons, kale, eggplant, green beans, squash, and an array of gorgeous flowers and succulents. When her remarkable garden was invaded by the neighborhood opossum family one night and its contents plundered, her response was, "I better figure out a better system for protecting the vegetables." She never said, "My garden is doomed! Fate won't allow tomatoes to survive here!" She owned the challenge of creating a garden that could thrive despite nightly visits from these destructive bandits, of maintaining a garden that was not only beautiful but also safe for her dogs (without traps or poison). She assumed that she had reasonable control over the outcome. She did her research and engineered new opossum-proof coverings for her planting beds.

Having an internal versus external locus of control isn't about a right way or wrong way of looking at things. Where we are on the continuum is based on personality, mindset, and experiences. However, studies have identified correlations between someone's locus of control and factors such as mood, anxiety, and level of optimism. Step Two—identifying the things you can control—will likely be more challenging for someone with a more external locus of control. We'll coach you with lots of examples, but if you find you are an extreme externalizer, you may benefit from some professional guidance in the form of counseling to help you learn ways to identify what you can control. It just comes more naturally to some than to others. Do not despair.

As you now know, Step One (the thumb of the hand, so to speak) involves getting a grip on your circumstances. It challenges you to stop self-medicating or escaping with alcohol or video games and to reach beyond simply acknowledging what your situation is, to identify what your life crisis is triggering from deep within you. It is the process of unearthing the past experiences that may in some way be amplifying your body's physical and emotional response to your current situation. Step Two (the pointer finger) involves pinpointing what you can control.

Step Two explores three questions about your crisis:

1. What can't I control?
2. What can I control?
3. What can I do about the things I can't control?

In a moment of crisis, our brains are wired to focus *only* on the crisis. Think back to "The Science of Stress" chapter's explanation of fight-or-flight: when suddenly faced with a bear, your entire system is focused on the split-second mechanisms of survival—blood pressure, oxygen delivery, muscle tension, reaction time. Your mind isn't about to start an internal debate over whether you should select tennis shoes for running or steel-toed boots for kicking. It is this telescopic focus on imminent danger that keeps us alive. Since humans are wired for acute, not chronic, crisis, taking a step back to evaluate the situation often doesn't come instinctively. Our brains are wired to be pulled to— and focused on—the threat. It is how we survive an acute crisis. We have to mentally override this system during times of chronic crisis, which takes some effort.

There's another reason why exploring what we *can* control is often difficult under pressure. It has to do with attitude and outlook, which are often molded by our social circles and communities, and even our shared culture. Think about the different television sitcoms you may have loved over the years: *Seinfeld*, *Friends*, *The Big Bang Theory*, *Schitt's Creek*. Every popular situation comedy shares a few common denominators: comedic timing, cast chemistry, and, oftentimes, sarcasm. Sarcasm is literally the backbone of much of our comedic entertainment. It's why we love Elaine Benes, Chandler Bing, Sheldon Cooper, and David Rose. Alanis Morissette's song "Ironic" is iconic because it hits that sarcastic button perfectly. Who hasn't had a black fly in her chardonnay? In a sense, that song unites us in the shared experiences of life's little miseries— ironically (pun intended), within the context of a catchy tune. (If you're my age, I know you're singing it in your head now.) It's a song that celebrates catastrophe, and we loved it enough that it was nominated for two Grammy Awards and two MTV Video Music Awards. In a crisis, however, sarcasm can take on another life-form, morphing from twisted humor to perceived reality, resulting in pessimistic thinking. And too much pessimistic thinking can pull a vulnerable mind (we're already focused on the crisis, right?) farther into the abyss. This also makes identifying what we can control more challenging, so it may be easiest if we start at the point of least resistance: identifying what we *can't* control. These things are just more likely to be lurking at the surface of your consciousness than the things you can control. Plus, humans tend to want to complain before moving to problem-solving (no judgment, friends), so let's just start here. We'll use Nina as our example.

What Can't Nina Control?

In Step One, you learned about Nina's predicament. On the surface, there's not much Nina can control about her situation. Already vulnerable from her own health problems, issues in her marriage, and the juggling of the joys and frustrations of raising teenagers, she's now crushed by her father's terminal cancer diagnosis. Digging deeper (in Step One), we found Nina has always relied on her father for emotional (and sometimes financial) support, to an extent that a somewhat codependent relationship evolved. She's now swimming in the cauldron of her own life's problems, suddenly faced with an enormous loss with meanings on so many levels beyond what an outsider would see and the task of figuring out how to take care of her father while living with her husband and teenagers in another city.

The first question Nina needs to consider is, what *can't* I control in this situation?

WHAT NINA CAN'T CONTROL:

- Her own health issues
- Her husband's "escaping into work"
- Teenagers
- Dad's cancer diagnoses, prognosis, course, or outcome
- Where she lives
- The future—how she'll cope down the line without her dad*

---

* If your gut is telling you Nina actually *can* control how she'll cope down the line, your instinct is right. However, for her to start imagining future scenarios (a son's wedding, the possible failure of her marriage, losing her job) and then trying to figure out how she is going to cope without her dad's advice or financial support in those scenarios is counterproductive and encourages catastrophic thinking—inventing the worst outcome in a lose-lose game of "what ifs." The point is, Nina can't control the future at all, nor can she accurately predict how she'll feel facing various potential life circumstances without her dad. In this moment, the future is not under her control.

- Dad's diagnosis triggering her own worries about her future health and aging, questions about whether she will inherit this cancer.

What *Can* Nina Control in This Situation?

Sometimes what you can or can't control is obvious. But it really pays to do a deeper dive here, past the obvious. It's helpful to grab a pen and notebook for this step and to write down all the things you *can* control, even if you're just going to throw the list away. It takes a lot of positive reinforcement to override a single negative event, and writing helps cement ideas into our brains. The purpose is to turn down the volume of—and eventually override—the internal alarm coursing through your veins by training your mind to look beyond the surface of the crisis. We're challenging that feeling of helplessness to a duel.

Nina can't control the cancer, but she can control her communication with her dad and his doctors. She can have her dad sign consent forms so she can communicate with his treatment team directly to help facilitate appointments and understand treatment options. She can open a dialog with her dad regarding his questions, his worries, and what he thinks about his situation. She can ask about his wishes and encourage him to make advanced health directives so his wishes can be followed even if he becomes unable to express them later. It isn't easy, but now is the time to discuss end-of-life issues. Does he want to be in his own home with in-home care? Does his insurance cover this? Will he need to be in a care home? Will he benefit from hospice care? Can any of those things be done in Nina's city? Nina can encourage her dad to make his own end-of-life decisions ahead of time so that when he is so ill he can't contribute to medical discussions, she can rest assured she's making decisions that would make him comfortable. If Nina's dad is in a panic and doesn't want to talk about any of it, Nina has done her part in bringing it up and can bring it up from time to time with help from his doctors and nurses. If he refuses to discuss any of these decisions, then his lack of a decision *is* his decision, and it is out of Nina's hands, onto the list of things not within her control. But initiating communication is.

This is the time for Nina to call a family meeting. It's an opportunity to talk to the kids about what is going on with their grandfather and what she's going through (and what one day they, too, may face) and to try to bring the family together as a team. Nina can talk about having to travel to help with her dad's care, about her stress and sorrow, and she can ask for support. This is a time when the family will be tested a little, and they'll manage best if each of them can be flexible and contribute to the running of the household. Nina can ask her teens what they're willing to do to help the family. Will one of them cook a few meals? Will they do their own laundry? Take out the trash? Feed the dog?

This is also a good time for Nina to talk to her husband about his tendency to escape into work and to ask him whether he's willing to cut back to take care of the family. It's also a time to identify the nonnegotiables that must be done and what can be put on hold for a while. Now isn't the time to let the contractor start the renovation, no matter how prepared he says he is to finish the project or how smoothly he thinks it is going to go. Nina (and her family, by extension) will be faced with things she can't even anticipate at this moment, so she needs to be kind to herself and put the nonessentials on hold, *without feeling guilty about it.*

Nina *can* take control of her schedule. (An old-fashioned paper calendar or weekly planner can be really helpful here, but so can a shared family digital calendar.) She can write out her teens' weekly schedules and reach out to the parents of their friends and ask for help driving them to school, sports, and other activities. She can ask friends or neighbors to prepare a meal for the freezer so that as Nina comes and goes the family has some home-cooked food. She can meet with her human resources department at work and discuss the policy for emergency leave (under the Family and Medical Leave Act, or FMLA, in the United States). How much paid time off does she have? Can she use sick days? Would the company allow other employees to donate their sick days?

Nina has control of her body. She is in control of her sleep schedule (prioritizing eight or nine hours every night) and her quality of sleep. Stress impinges on sleep, but by cutting out any caffeine ten hours before her bedtime, sticking with her sleep/wake schedule every day of the week (10 P.M. to 7 A.M., for example), and not exercising, eating, or drinking late at night, she is making healthy decisions that will maximize her sleep quality.

She is also in control of her fuel—what she eats. Fast food and junk food often provide some sort of momentary comfort, but they can lead to mood swings and energy crashes. I practice in Southern California, where the streets are inundated with high-end performance cars, so I sometimes ask a patient, "What goes into the gas tank of a Porsche?" The answer is always the same: high-octane fuel. The car won't function well if you put sludge into the tank. Why would a human be different? Fuel matters. With a little planning, Nina can ensure that she has access to healthy fuel during her crisis. She can stock up on nuts, fruits, and vegetables, and she can schedule a little time for advanced cooking. One hour on a quiet Sunday afternoon will give her a dozen servings of a hearty and healthy vegetable chicken soup to freeze and use in the coming weeks ahead. She can also cut down on alcohol.

LET'S HAVE A BRIEF DISCUSSION ABOUT WHY ALCOHOL IS A FAKE FRIEND

Some people turn to alcohol to relax, but alcohol is actually a "frenemy" of a life crisis. In the moment it can calm you down, but it can also disinhibit you. Someone with a happy demeanor is typically more happy with alcohol, but someone who is angry or irritable can become more so. Even when alcohol has a calming effect, it doesn't last long. Alcohol is a central nervous system depressant. As the body metabolizes it, it has the opposite effect, and the nervous system becomes more stimulated. The effect tends to be proportional to the amount consumed, but even small amounts of alcohol to unwind can lead to a delayed stimulation of the central nervous system, resulting in restless sleep, waking during the night, and exaggerated anxiety responses the following day.

Nina can also control her access to fresh air and exercise. As stressed as she is, she can take two or three minutes to step outside, listen to the air blowing through the trees, and feel the sunshine on her skin. Or maybe she'll smell rain and feel the crispness of the air or be wrapped in humidity. It is important to regularly take a few minutes and just be in the moment, focusing thoughts only on the sensations present, with worries intentionally put aside for a few minutes.

Nina can also choose movement over stagnation. As busy as she is, she can take the stairs, park far away, and walk a little more, or make a habit of going for a fifteen-minute walk as soon as she arrives home from work or while running errands at the mall. Exercise—and brief is better than none—is one of the best nonpharmaceutical treatments for stress, depression, impaired sleep, and poor focus. Even when it feels impossible to fit it in, adding a fifteen-minute walk sometime during the day is almost always possible.

Most importantly, Nina can control her thoughts. During times when nothing in life seems to be in control, the one thing we can always control is *what* and *how* we are thinking. It's beautifully powerful. Let's step away from Nina for a minute to discuss.

Thoughts, Flexibility, and Attitude

Our thoughts and feelings seem to be coupled by some sort of subconscious pinky-swear to always stick together. The human brain looks for external justification for the internal emotional state. Humans are wired for consistency, and our brains don't like discrepancies. Studies show that people with depressed brains tend to slide into pessimistic outlooks, resulting in a perceived balance between the outside and inside environments. In other words, when we're sad we prefer cloudy skies, so we feel the universe is gloomy, too. Sunny days often make depression worse because we feel disconnected from the surrounding environment. The psychological term for this is positivity-negativity bias. It is the brain's tendency to enhance things that are positive in the environment (optimistic thinking) or magnify the negative.

Understanding this helps us take a step back. If my life situation has left me feeling angry, depressed, anxious, or helpless, what are my thoughts like? It's important to pay attention to your running commentary of thoughts. Is the tone negative? Sarcastic? Angry? Resentful? What is your imagination conjuring up? My patient Ellen said this:

> I was driving into the office today for our appointment, and a car cut in front of me. Nothing happened, but in

my mind I started imagining he hit me, and for twenty minutes, I drove along like a zombie, lost in my imagining of all sorts of horrible outcomes—needing an ambulance, being in pain, having my car towed—and the consequences of those outcomes—being on crutches, not having a car to drive to work and school, the financial burdens it would cause. I literally spent the entire drive thinking of one horrible scenario after another. It was strange to arrive here and find myself... myself. Why do I do that? It feels awful.

Ellen's stressed brain was looking for external reasons to be stressed. When it couldn't find any on the gloriously sunny morning, it decided to create something, which magnified the intensity of her stressed emotional state further. Ellen's brain felt justified, but the price she paid wasn't worth it.

It is uncomfortable to challenge a thought pattern that is congruent with one's internal emotional state. The brain doesn't like the discrepancy. But changing what you think is an important step in changing how you feel. Now that Ellen has started recognizing and paying attention to the content of her imagination, she can choose whether she wishes to continue with a fantasy or cut it off, put on some music, roll down the window, and feel the sunshine and breeze on her skin as she drives.

One option is to create a mantra or a motto. A friend of mine encountered several threats at once—he lost his job, the unhealthy aspects of his long-term relationship were surfacing, and he and his boyfriend were going to have to move out of their home. He was faced with the possible loss of everything familiar, so I encouraged him to pick a "word of the year" to help shape his outlook. He texted a few ideas: *hope, strength, patience, faith.* "FAITH!!!!!" was my reply with that many exclamation points, followed by a series of GIFs of George Michael wiggling his bottom and the YouTube link to his "Faith" video. His word of the year came with its own built-in theme song. What could be more perfect? When he felt himself sliding into pessimism, he could choose to pull up the song on his phone, crank up the volume, and dance around his bedroom. If it sounds ridiculous, good. Ridiculous can teach the brain an important lesson: *I can override that negativity bias you're throwing at me with a little wiggle of my (or George Michael's) bottom.*

Another patient of mine came in for her first appointment and stated, "I can't sleep. It's the worst thing. I haven't slept for years, and no one can help me." Well, that's not a loaded sentence, is it? She has just declared her belief that she is untreatable. Since mindset plays such a big role in life, if she believes it, she will own it and run with it. Thoughts like that can become a person's identity. The truth is, every living thing (that I know of, anyway) sleeps. Birds, fish, bears, and baby goats are just like humans: we all sleep. Sleep may be disrupted, interrupted, or of poor quality due to external or internal circumstances (screaming babies, sleep apnea, etc.), but sleep happens. Unless this patient changes her mindset, even after sleeping a few hours, she will continue to feel the same emotional pain. The internal dialog needs to be updated. "Eventually, I'm going to sleep. Not sleeping isn't the worst thing; it will just make me tired, and no one ever died of being tired."

If you aren't a "motto" kind of person, it can also help you to focus on the big picture. You may be suffering through a divorce that would top the list of the world's most contentious divorces, but the heaviness can start lifting every time you remind yourself you're willing to pay the price required to separate from the person who has so mistreated you. You can change your mindset from victim to master of your own fate. You can't control your ex in a divorce, but you can focus on how glad you are that this person is no longer in your bed. You control the content of your thoughts and your attitude.

Back to Nina. Let's summarize what she *can* control.

What Nina Can Control

- Communication with her dad and his treatment team
- Encouragement of advanced health directives
- The simplification and organization of her schedule
- Reaching out to friends and neighbors for help
- Organizing ahead of time to make last-minute trips easier
- Talk to the human resources department at work about options for leave
- Her sleep schedule
- What she eats
- Whether she makes time for exercise, fresh air, and meditation
- Her thoughts, attitude, and flexibility

What Can I Do About the Things I Can't Control?

The final component of Step Two involves asking this question: what can I do about the things I can't control? The purpose of this component is to start chipping away at that pesky feeling of helplessness that sometimes creeps up. If I can't control it, what are my options here? If you're struggling to get started, ask a good friend to brainstorm with you. Some of her ideas may work and some may irritate you, but it's a starting point to get your creative juices flowing at a time when your creativity may be hibernating. It's like cowriting a book with a Norwegian. When I get stuck, I call or text him. He doesn't have all the answers, but his brain works differently enough to get me out of my rut and help me start thinking with a fresh perspective. It's sometimes helpful to have some input from someone who isn't "in" your life crisis. It isn't about having someone tell you what you should do; it's about inviting a different perspective and possibly looking at your options from a new angle.

Earlier, we outlined the things that Nina can't control in her situation, including her own health issues and her dad's prognosis. What can she do about them? While Nina can't change the course of some of her chronic health issues, she can certainly have regular appointments with her doctor and actually follow the medical advice she's given. (That sounds so simple, but how many of us delay going in for bloodwork, getting a prostate exam, a colonoscopy, a mammogram, etc.?) She can ask her doctor whether her dad's cancer tends to be hereditary and whether there are steps she can start taking now to improve her health. She certainly can't control her teenagers, but she can open lines of communication with them and with her spouse, too, and she can encourage everyone to "hit the reset button" together moving forward. She can go to a grief support group or even a see a therapist to address the deeply rooted fears her father's illness is unearthing. She can talk to the social worker at the hospital and inquire about resources, hospice care, and what his insurance will cover. Addressing each of these options chips away at Nina's feelings of helplessness piece by piece.

As you start to think about your own Step Two and ask yourself the three questions, remember: this step involves *pinpointing* options, not committing to acting on them. You are not creating a ginormous to-do list. You are training your brain to step

beyond reacting to your crisis. You are designing a measure of
control over your circumstances, boldly challenging that sense
of helplessness that creeps in. Inventing options. My favorite
synonym for *option* is *possibility*. What is possible for you?

Step Three:
Push into Motion

Kjell Tore

I N PHYSICS, NEWTON'S FAMOUS FIRST law of motion states
that an object remains unmoved until an external force acts
on it. In a crisis, stress can knock you out so bad you feel like an
object being acted on by a hellish chaos of external forces; all
you can do is react. Your ex-spouse serves you with legal papers;
you react. Your employer tells you to get to work or be fired; you
react. Your fourteen-year-old tells you she is going to spend the
weekend with a friend—and, by the way, it's in Las Vegas; you
react. Whatever the scenario, reacting to other people's behavior means that someone else is in control—like the lake rippling
in response to a rock being thrown into it or a tree shaking and
then falling when chopped repeatedly by an ax.

In case you didn't notice, feeling like an object doesn't feel
very good. It can make you feel humiliated, abused, worthless,
and worse. That's what "lack of control" does to you. The lake
and the trees, when shaken, have an easier time of it because

they don't have an inner universe of thoughts ("what ifs"...),
feelings (fears...), and emotions (pride...) to grapple with, they
just ripple or fall and that's the end of it. You may even feel that
rippling and falling are good alternatives, but the good news is
that you have the power to take control of the situation and put
action into motion to set things straight.

The key to gaining a feeling of control is to get moving on
implementing the actions you decide are needed to fix your
problem.

Remember the earlier steps: ready (Get a Grip—thumb), set
(Pinpoint What You Can Control—pointer finger), now get
poised to...Go! The first two steps are just preparation. Now
give your problems the middle finger with Push into Motion!
Steps One and Two in the previous chapters describe how to
start the process of taking control over your mind and body
when a crisis strikes. By reining in your focus, naming the problem, and pinpointing what you can control and can't control,
you press the pause button on your escalating crisis and create
a space in which to start the work needed to quiet the noise.

Imagine yourself as a pilot who feels like hitting the eject button at the first sign of lightning and thunder ahead. The eject
response is natural and automatic. You might even think *Problem
solved...*, but then comes the gnawing realization that you
would eject yourself out of the plane with all the passengers—
family, friends, and colleagues—still up in the air, but now
without a pilot. Whoops! That was not your intention, and that
is not the action that is going to heal you. So you need to learn
to Get a Grip and Pinpoint at the first sign of a crisis so you don't
bail at the first sign of trouble, then follow up by taking the actions needed to stabilize your path through the storm. You are
the pilot in your life, and you need to get into the cockpit, where
all the controls are!

After having worked through the first two chapters, it's time to Push into Motion the actions that will help get you through your storm.

Step Three: Push into Motion

Steps 1 and 2 were the preparation: Like an Olympic athlete at the gate of the freestyle mogul race, you've integrated your focus and identified the path ahead. Now it's time to rock and roll! This Push into Motion step needs more than optimistic words, smiley faces, and best wishes; you need to be motivated and committed to tackle whatever jumps, bumps, and hairpin turns the course has in store for you. Four elements will push in motion the work needed for you to take control of your crisis.

1. Find your inner motivation.
2. Embrace positivity.
3. Divide tasks into Easy and Tough Actions.
4. Transition from thinking to acting.

Let's take a look at each element.

Find Your Inner Motivation

In professional sports, you need to have tremendous inner drive and motivation to keep you on track through countless hours of practice and through the physical and emotional pain of injuries and setbacks. But we need inner drive and motivation in our everyday lives as well. We need drive and motivation to get up in the morning, to get to work on time, and to walk across the street to the market for food (and chocolate).

The mind has built-in drive and motivation to do or get the basics—food, water, snuggles, rest. Some things are more urgent and motivating than others. But how can we find the inner drive and motivation to help us reach the bigger targets we set for ourselves, like staying on track while working through our crisis, finishing college, or curtailing habits we know are not good for us (like abusing drugs or alcohol)?

I asked Jennifer, who is a specialist in addiction medicine, to describe in concrete steps how she works with patients to find inner motivation for behavior change.

A Few Words from Jennifer on Motivation

No offense to Newton and his first law, but it only applies to objects, not human behavior. We don't have to wait for an outside influence to get us going. For change to be lasting, motivation needs to be internal. My patients have to stop using drugs when *they* decide it's time; they can apply to grad school only after *they* sign up for and take the GRE test. What stops us from doing the things we want to do? Well, sometimes we don't want to do them. Humans are sometimes torn between wanting to get off the roller coaster of drugs and loving the rush; a fear of failure (or a fear of success) may be the subconscious hesitation that makes us miss the deadline for signing up for the exam.

How do I address ambivalence with patients? While there are a number of "motivational enhancement" techniques, I like to use what I call the "four grid experiment."

Let's say Adrianne is in an unhealthy marriage and is working the Five Steps. In Step One, she came to terms with how verbally and emotionally abusive her spouse is. He is intimidating, controlling, dishonest, and a regular drinker. He is routinely unfaithful. Her underlying issue is that she is very religious and her church teaches divorce is a sin.

Her Step Two might be: Adrianne can't control her spouse's behavior, but she can control her own and her reactions to him, and she can talk to a therapist before contemplating separation.

Adrianne's heart and her therapist both agree this relationship is devastating to her well-being, but she still feels ambivalent about filing for divorce because of guilt. She is frozen, unable to move forward.

This is where I pull out a single piece of paper and divide it into four quadrants. The top left is labeled "Benefits of Divorce," the top right is "Consequences of Divorce," and the bottom left is "Benefits of Staying Married," and the bottom right is "Consequences of Staying Married." The four grids help give a visual, and I encourage my patients to fill in the boxes with any and every argument they can think of for each box.

Adrianne's Benefits of Divorce:	Adrianne's Consequences of Divorce:
No more sleeping with an abuser	Possible judgment from friends, family, and her faith community
Feeling safe at home	The church's reaction
No more surprise STDs	Fear she can't support herself on her own
Not having to live in constant fear	
Adrianne's Benefits of Staying Married:	**Adrianne's Consequences of Staying Married:**
She believes marriage is forever	Ongoing abuse, lies, and cheating
Financial stability	Ongoing intolerable anxiety
She stays in her life's routine	Regular STD testing
No guilt for leaving	Living with an alcoholic who won't get help
Spouse is usually nice when he's sober	

Once the grids are filled in, I hand my patient a highlighter and have him or her highlight the three most important items on the page. It gives a powerful visual. Adrianne realizes feeling safe at home and not living in constant fear far outweigh the consequences of ongoing abuse, dishonesty, and cheating. In other words, she sees that she values her well-being more than she hates divorce. She doesn't have to like divorce or want divorce in order to file for divorce: she just has to want peace and safety more.

Step Three is about tapping into your inner strength, your resolve, your fighting spirit; it's finding the fire in your belly to make changes to get you through this crisis.

You may feel frozen by a new diagnosis of lung disease; motivation may come from deciding you value life above smoking. You may live an organic, all-natural life, but when your oncologist tells you chemotherapy is the only option, you may decide being around for your children's future is more important to you than this chemical exposure. Motivation is found when we take a step back and evaluate our beliefs and desires and then decide one decision simply outweighs another. My patients don't go into treatment until they discover they want to live more than they want to get high. They don't apply to grad school until they decide the desire for courage and achievement outweighs inner fears. Hate whatever crisis has brought you to this book, but love something more than you hate your crisis, and use the thing you love or value as your motivation.

Jennifer's grid scheme makes a lot of sense. You need to be clear about the change you want to make and the benefits of achieving that change, and then use those positives to drive your commitment to that change. The largest hindrance to change is the fear of change itself; the easiest choice is always to not change anything and continue on as before. Find the inner motivation to overpower any fear of change. The chances that a drug addict keeps using or an anorexic continues to starve herself are sky high since that is what he or she knows and does well. It doesn't much matter that the behavior seems destructive and bizarre to people looking at the behavior from the outside; for the addict or anorexic, it is completely logical and familiar. For any lasting change to occur, however, the motivation for the individual to change will have to come from within.

The same is true for you to make a change: it's up to you to find the inner strength to take the actions needed to fight your crisis. It's within your control. And if you want to make a change but can't make it happen on your own, then reach out for help. The job of a psychiatrist, psychologist, and therapist is to help guide you through the changes you decide are right for you in your life.

Embrace Positivity

In any endeavor, if you want to change or improve, being positive and optimistic is the secret sauce. You may be rolling your eyes right now. Wearing rose-colored glasses and thinking everything is going to be all right isn't going to solve your problem, is it? Well, not so fast. Just trust me.

Of course, nobody likes to be around a grumpy person. Think about it. A teen who says *no* to anything you suggest doing, an old fogey complaining incessantly about aches and pains, the midlifer talking about how everything was better thirty years ago, and the know-it-all who is convinced everyone else is an idiot and only he has the right answers—their grumpiness sucks the energy out of the people around them.

I had a patient in his late seventies who had to move into a nursing home because he was alone and not able to care for himself. The house he had built with his own two hands was sold, his driver's license was taken away, and his cherished dog—who he had walked every day—was adopted by a neighbor. Obviously, this was a miserable turn of events that turned his earlier independent and active life upside down. Whenever his granddaughter came to visit, he would talk for hours about everything he could no longer do and how miserable he was. Understandably, the granddaughter started visiting him less and less often. Sure, the grandfather needed to talk to someone about all the negative thoughts he was struggling with, but that was the only thing he would ever talk to his granddaughter about. The girl would come over, and my patient would just dump everything on her. The grandfather was just so overwhelmed by his situation that he could not regulate his urge to continually talk about his miserable luck. By becoming aware of it, finding a better outlet for his complaints, and learning better strategies to regulate his thoughts, mood and attitude, he regained a positive circle of contact with his grandchild.

But our attitude and outlook don't affect just those around us. They also have a profound impact on our own well-being. My friend Carl is the perfect example of a person who always sees the glass half full and not half empty. A constant source of potential irritation for him is his ex-wife, who never misses an opportunity for biting sarcasm after their son has been with his father. She calls Carl a "circus dad" because he regularly does something special with his son, like camping in the forest, making waffles outdoors after a long ski trip, or attending a children's play at the local historical museum. Carl knows the mother is struggling with health issues that impact her mood, so when she serves up snarky comments to him, Carl takes it in stride and tries to turn the conversation into something positive. He compliments her on her efforts to give their son good habits, regular routines, and healthy practices without sounding condescending. And he looks for ways to help make her life easier. Carl knows that going down into the trenches and lobbing insults back and forth is not going to benefit his son. Being positive and friendly in the face of hostility boosts his self-confidence and enhances a feeling of being in control. And he knows that any other strategy would just give him a headache. He consciously takes the half-full approach at every potential emotional trigger. He is my inspiration on a daily basis.

I think it's easy to understand that people in a miserable situation can become grumpy even if they never have been that way before, but actively working to be a positive force, whatever your situation, is a smart life philosophy: it will energize you and everyone around you.

Now, you might think it unfair of me to say you should be positive in the middle of your crisis, but let me offer you these three points:

First of all, positive feelings and energy elicit positive responses from others. I try to practice this every day. I smile at people walking toward me on the street, and they smile back. This is more common in California than in Europe, and it's one reason my European friends love visiting the United States. A German friend visiting California thought all the cashiers at the supermarket were in love with him because they smiled at him and asked him how he was doing. So, yes, there are cultural differences. But so what; feeling loved is a good thing. It always makes me feel good to smile at people and see their stern faces light up with a smile as they pass me by. Feeling good yourself and making others feel good is better than the alternative. So purposely being positive in your expression, your tone, and your words even when in crisis mode—literally putting a smile on your face—not only makes those around you feel better, it also lifts your mood.

Second, you are more creative when you are positive. Positive energy allows you to think in more novel and productive ways to conceptualize and achieve goals. Research has shown that positive employees are more creative, more effective, and enjoy their work more. When you are working to improve your situation, a negative mood will activate fear processes that limit your scope and narrow your focus, while a positive mood will widen your field of view and open up more alternatives, opportunities, and possibilities.

Third, people who are positive are more self-confident and think more positively about themselves. The psychological term *self-efficacy* is an important element in successful individuals: it refers to believing in yourself and in your skills and abilities. A good example is that of professional athletes who spend a lifetime building self-confidence through practice. If a downhill skier in a competition doesn't think she is going to make it down the hill standing, chances are she won't. (Her body preps her for falling.) The same is true for the rest of us in our daily lives. If I think a relationship will fail, the way I interpret signs and signals in my partner will increase the likelihood of it failing. I know my chances for success are much higher when I think positively and believe in myself. The relationship may fail anyway, but at least I gave it my best shot. I can only control myself, not others and external factors, but I am more likely to make it down the hill standing up if I believe I will succeed.

Like athletes, we, too, can practice positivity and use techniques to boost our performance under stressful conditions. One effective mental technique athletes use is selective memory. They remember their good performances that build their self-confidence and not their bad ones. There is a famous story about a legendary golfer who was interviewed by a journalist about an upcoming tournament. He was asked if he was worried about his putting going into an upcoming weekend tournament since he had missed several short putts the week before. He looked confident and said he had never missed a putt under six feet in his career. The journalist challenged him and wanted to show him videos of several four-foot misses the week before. The legend ignored the journalist, repeating that he had never missed a putt under six feet in his career. Next question! No reason for him to put thoughts of failure in his head. The lesson is this: keep the successes that give you confidence well in your thoughts and leave the others outside the door to cool off.

Faith is also an undervalued tool. Not being a very religious person, I could never quite understand the amazing power of faith. In my first year at university, a fellow student who was very religious was trying to convince me he could move mountains if he wanted to. There were mountains surrounding the entire campus, so I asked him to choose any one of them and show me his stuff. I never saw him move any mountain, but thinking back, I was amazed at his self-confidence. He believed with all his heart that if he wanted to, he could.

Thinking about it now, I see this faith in himself as a superpower, whether he ever actually moved a mountain or not. When I'm working with young individuals in the depths of despair and depression, with absolutely no scaffolding of self-esteem or self-confidence to prop them up, I wish I could fill them with the power of an inspiring faith—in themselves and their own abilities, with the confidence in themselves to move mountains, too.

Have faith in yourself to get through your crisis. Find inspiration in people who have faith in their futures and use the same type of drive to power your journey.

Divide Tasks into Easy and Tough Actions

Get into a positive mindset before taking on the Easy and Tough Actions you need to get the job done; it will give you wind in your sails, grease the wheels of action, and improve your chances of getting the best outcome. But why divide your pinpointed to-dos into Easy and Tough Actions?

The reason is that in a crisis, it's easy to feel overwhelmed and not get anything done at all. In times of crisis, you may need to deal with many things at once and there is a natural tendency to shift into default mode and simply react to incoming requirements. And if those things are the biggest and most complex tasks and you try to tackle them first, it might take the wind out of your sails so that you don't get anything done at all. So start with Easy Actions.

Dividing all the issues into Easy and Tough Actions will help you choose a starting point that is consistent with your current energy level and to set the ball rolling to build yourself up to deal with more complicated tasks ahead.

The other day, my mind and heart crashed when I got news that a former patient had taken his own life. I was utterly devastated. My mind became consumed by thoughts of what I could or should have done differently and what his family was going through. For days, I felt paralyzed and unable to get anything done with the many current patients I was treating. I didn't know where to start.

I started by dividing up all of the urgent things I needed to do in the next week into Easy and Tough Actions. Among the Easy Actions were to get to sleep at the right time, eat regularly, keep to my exercise routine, pick up my youngest son from school on schedule, and get to work on time. These easier actions could be done with less mental effort.

The more difficult actions required more mental effort and involved getting an overview of the events leading up to the tragedy, speaking to the man's family, preparing to answer questions they might have, and writing a eulogy his family asked me to give at the funeral. I also reached out to colleagues for help in following up with patients I was treating who needed urgent care but I didn't have the time to see.

Getting started on Easy Actions would help me get some control over my focus and give me confidence in the face of the more emotionally challenging tasks. As I completed the easier tasks, I could then start on the difficult tasks that would require considerably more mental and emotional effort.

LET'S GET BACK to Nina and her crisis involving her father's diagnosis of cancer and the prognosis of him having just a few months to live. How did she divide up her actions?

NINA'S EASY ACTIONS
- Meals—time and content
- Routines for exercise, fresh air, quiet, intimacy/romance/sex
- Sleep schedule
- Communicating with her dad and doctors
- Reaching out to friends and neighbors for help

Nina started work on her list of Easy Actions that would allow her to quickly get into a regular routine. She was keenly aware of being positive in all interactions with her dad, her family, and the health personnel involved in her father's care. The most challenging of these Easy Actions was her sleep schedule, as she would often lie in bed for hours without getting to sleep. She looked into how she could organize her sleep routines to ensure better sleep habits and possibly discuss with her doctor ways to ensure a sounder sleep.

NINA'S TOUGH ACTIONS
- Getting treatment for physical health issues
- Talking to husband about him "escaping into work"
- Tackling financial issues such as travel to care for her father and the cost of health care
- Dealing with her teenage sons

· Addressing her growing alcohol dependence
· Seeking help for her bouts of anxiety and depression

The Tough Action list involved more complicated actions that would either take more time or require the involvement of other people. Beyond what Nina could do with regard to eating, sleeping, and living well, many of her physical health issues would have to be addressed in collaboration with various health care personnel. She trusted her primary care doctor and could work with her on dealing with one issue at a time.

Several issues, such as finances and her rebellious teenage sons, would ideally have to be worked on together with her husband. She would have to see whether he was willing to scale back his work schedule and get more involved in the day-to-day raising of their children. If not, she would have to figure out how to deal with these issues on her own or bring in others to help.

If she ended up escaping further into alcohol, all of the efforts that she was doing would be wasted. She needed to decide on fair rules for when and how often she had alcohol, if at all, and to agree with herself that if she broke the limits she set for herself she would seek professional help. Despite her efforts to be positive, if she continued to suffer bouts of anxiety and depression, this was also something that would spur her to contact a health professional to help her gain control over these emotions.

LET'S HAVE A BRIEF DISCUSSION ABOUT DELAY STRATEGIES

We are all experts at making excuses for not doing something today that we can put off until tomorrow. It can be delaying easy tasks such as cleaning up the kitchen and taking out the trash or tough tasks such as talking to a partner about sexual problems or reaching out for help to overcome substance abuse issues. Delay strategies are even more tempting when you are stressed. While working on this chapter, I realized I had developed a tendency to watch the news more than ever, avoiding what I needed to do to meet the deadline that my coauthor and I had set. It doesn't have anything to do with being smart or not. In fact, the smarter you are, the better you may be at thinking of excuses not to do something! It does have something to do with up-regulating your attentional focus to the matter at hand and down-regulating your focus on the millions of other much-more-fun things to do. Believe in or train your ability to delay gratification and you will be better prepared to avoid putting off what you need to do right now.

Transition from Thinking to Acting

The transformation of an idea in our head such as *I will go to bed at 11 P.M. tonight* to actually going to bed at 11 P.M. has always fascinated me—enough to spend four years of my life studying the transition of thing-in-head to thing-in-real-life and writing a doctoral thesis on the subject. For some, it's a matter of just thinking about alternatives and then acting on the best one. For others, it's not so easy. And it's certainly not easy for anybody during a crisis. So, I totally understand if you struggle to implement even the most basic Easy Action on your list.

In technical jargon, we call the ability to actually do what you are thinking about doing *executive control*. There are lots of great books on the subject, but in short, think of it like this: your brain is like a car full of thoughts and feelings inside, and your behavior is like a wagon hitched to the back of that car. While you are driving on a smooth highway, the car (thoughts and emotions) and the wagon (behavior) are relatively coordinated and moving in the same direction. But when you suddenly find yourself driving fast on a rocky dirt road with potholes everywhere (crisis!), the wagon jumps all over the place in relation to the car and may even become unhitched. Your thoughts are no longer in sync with your behavior despite your best intentions. I get it—and I see it every day in my practice. I have even experienced it myself.

Besides finding our inner motivation and embracing positivity, the true test of whether you are ready to Push into Motion and move on to the next steps is whether you are able to start doing Easy Actions on a daily basis. If not, don't worry. It may mean you need to work on building attentional focus (discussed in Step One), and/or find more basic Easy Actions to start with, and/or reach out to a friend or therapist for help and support. Don't give up and go back to the old behavior you want to change. Keep your mind and heart on your goal of aligning thinking feeling, and behaving in a smooth forward trajectory.

To RECAP, STEP THREE is about empowering you to start taking action so that you can regain control of your life. To begin this process, you need to:

- Find your inner motivation and be as positive as possible in your efforts.
- Start with Easy Actions and build your confidence for the Tough Actions.
- Transition from Thinking to Acting.

Finding your inner motivation and enhancing positivity will help you complete the actions needed to stabilize your crisis. Start with Easy Actions and then, when you are ready, move onto Tough Actions. But remember, putting thoughts into action is not always a straightforward process. It is influenced positively by good routines such as getting enough sleep, eating nutritious meals, and having healthy fun. It is negatively affected by stress, alcohol, and drug use. If you are not able to practice Easy Actions to help start your change process, don't despair. You may need some support, you may need to recalibrate your timeline, but you will get there. You've gotten this far. Keep your eyes on that glorious prize of changing your life for the better.

Step Four:
Pull Back

Jennifer

S OMETIMES I SEE A YELLOW bucket. No, I'm not one of those psychiatrists who experiments with LSD; it's just a visual thought that makes itself present in the space between me and a patient from time to time. The bucket is wide and very tall, filled with water. It represents my patient's tolerance for stress, and this picture comes to mind when I sense it full to the brim.

Many of us have a large capacity for dealing with stress, but once we reach capacity, the addition of even one tiny drop will spill over the edge, resulting in what scientists refer to as *losing our shit.** This can cause a lot of confusion for the person who just handed us a single drop. And we've probably all lost it at

---

* Not really a scientific term, but I use it all the time, and I'm a scientist, right?

some point over something really small, like the dog getting out, the milk being left on the counter, or someone squeezing the toothpaste tube from the "wrong" place. These "nothing" things, when one's stress bucket is full, can cause a cascade of emotions to spill over the fragile edge of the bucket, confusing and alienating the people in our lives.

At the bottom of the bucket is a spigot. When we figure out how to open it, we can start emptying some of the water from the bottom of the bucket, gradually creating more space for new stuff by clearing out the old. In this way, we increase our capacity for dealing with life's drama. It's like letting a little air out of an overfilled balloon or allowing that overly stretched rubber band to relax. This is Step Four. Following the intensity of action in Step Three and giving your crisis the middle finger, it's time for the ring finger—a symbol not of strength or power but of intimacy. The ring finger is personal. Now we turn inward.

Sometimes I think *self-care* is the new swear word in psychiatry. In my office, the term elicits everything from blank stares to eye rolls and cringes; long gone are the days when I'd mention it and someone's eyes would widen and face light up, as if something exciting were about to happen. Self-care has been hijacked by marketing firms to sell us everything from moisturizer to products for thinning hair and nasty toenails. For some people, it has become synonymous with a day at the spa or specialty health and beauty products you can only buy from your friend's Facebook page. But self-care isn't fluffy pampering or consumerism, and it has nothing to do with having a bikini wax—or trimming nose hair (but seriously... do that).

One week, three young adult siblings came to see me. Each had an individual appointment and was accompanied by the father, who had arranged for his kids' consultations. He had identified concerns with each—one used cannabis, one was stuck on video games for hours every night, one was the nicest

young woman on the planet but had a mean temper. Dad came
into the beginning of each appointment to share his concerns
before leaving us to it. On the third day, I finally asked when *he*
was coming to see me. My question surprised him, and he replied his kids were his priority and he wanted to get them sorted
first. However, I was concerned. Over the course of the week, I
had seen him several times, and each time he looked more pale
and exhausted than the time before. He dressed smartly and
wore a confident façade, but he wasn't fooling me. When he
didn't come in, I made a bold decision and called him. Something
was wrong.

He surprised me by agreeing to come in for a session. On his
intake paperwork, he listed anemia as a past medical problem,
so I asked him about it. "For some reason my hemoglobin runs
low," he said, "and when it gets too low, I have to get blood trans-
fusions. My doctor is on top of it."

"Are *you* on top of it?" I asked.

He paused, then said, "I'm due for a transfusion, but I wanted
to bring my kids here first." He admitted that his hemoglobin
had actually fallen dangerously low and that his doctor had ordered him in for a transfusion, but he thought it perfectly
normal to fly to California for a week so his kids could have
these consultations with me first. "They're my priority."

I was both incredulous and alarmed. "You can die from low
hemoglobin," I told him. "You can have a stroke, heart failure,
organ damage. If you don't take care of yourself, you won't be
able to take care of your kids." He promised to see his doctor
right away.

A few weeks later, I called him to check in. "I have to drive
the kids to their games. They have homework. Every night, I
cook dinner. My wife travels for work. I just can't go in!" I could
hardly believe my ears. This man was allowing himself to die a
slow death because he wouldn't stop the busyness for one after-

noon to get his transfusion, putting his future in jeopardy. Which is really more important: one afternoon of basketball or a future playing with your grandkids?

Although this man's situation was extreme, many of us have some version of it in our lives during a crisis. We put off taking care of ourselves because it feels like everything around us is a fire that needs to be put out. Kids need to be fed. Endless laundry needs to be put away. The dog is encrusted with a mysterious goo, and when asked about, it the children all suddenly have amnesia. The *last* thing on our minds is self-care. It sounds like a time-sucking luxury we just can't afford.

Step Four is about *real* self-care. It is a time of reflection. Simplification. Of evaluating how we treat ourselves. Setting intentions. Letting some of the water out of the bucket. It's the private journey of self-intimacy, which is an important part of moving forward through a crisis.

STEP FOUR INVOLVES FOUR (FIVE,* ACTUALLY) MAIN PRINCIPLES

1. Reflection and simplification
2. Evaluating how you treat yourself
3. Setting intentions
4. Self-intimacy

---

* Mindfulness is the key to starting the engine of Step Four.

First, we need to calm the complete tornado of the million thoughts and feelings swishing around inside us.

Mindfulness—
The Panacea for Catastrophic Thinking

OK, it isn't actually a panacea, but hear me out. When we're stressed, our thoughts tend to alternate between ruminating on past events and worrying about the future. We aren't always *present*. I can't tell you how many people have come into my office worried about dementia because they keep losing their keys, forgetting to buy items at the market, forgetting names, and missing exits on the freeway. Occasionally, I diagnose people with dementia, but more often I diagnose them with anxiety. The reality is, most of these people aren't losing their keys; they're simply not paying attention to what they're doing when they put them down. Their minds are elsewhere. They zone out, missing details and hardly noticing the life going on around them because they're stuck in their heads. It's good news, actually, because it's a lot easier to treat anxiety than dementia. But stress is a grand mimicker of many other problems, causing people to run to the doctor to be evaluated for attention deficit disorder, Alzheimer's disease, chest pain, and digestive issues.

When we're stressed, our brains look for ongoing justification for it, and if there isn't stress in the moment, our minds will take us elsewhere—even to our imaginations, where we *invent* reasons to be stressed. The slow and steady treatment for this is mindfulness. Mindfulness is a fancy term for being in the moment—in *this* moment, right here, right now. Not in the past, not worrying about tomorrow. Here.

What's so special about the here and now, when I'm sitting with my hair in a bun wearing pig slippers? It offers a hidden escape from your crisis. When you have thirty minutes before bed all to yourself, which is better: ruminating on the day's events and cementing the guilt of all your imperfections into your brain lobes or lighting a candle and opening a book? The answer is obvious, but how many of us don't actually choose the thing that will benefit us? Telling yourself *In this moment now, all I need to do is read this book* gives your brain a much-needed break from constant overprocessing. It also starts training it not to live in constant worry. You can do the same thing when cooking dinner. Instead of worrying about your upcoming court case or your mom's doctor appointment, pretend you're on *Top Chef* and focus on your chopping, mixing, and flavor profiles. Get lost in the experience. Worrying in this moment isn't going to solve some massive legal problem or alter the course of your mom's chemotherapy. But stopping the worrying in this moment will begin a forward momentum in your brain toward rejuvenation. It offers a respite from overthinking.

Reflection and Simplification

Once you've practiced being in the here and now, you can bring in reflection and simplification. Ask yourself, how am I adding stress to my life? A patient of mine was in a contentious divorce that resulted in serious financial strain. She was so angry at her ex that she didn't want to budge on anything. She insisted on going on the same vacations, keeping the kids in their private schools, leasing the same expensive car, and maintaining all of their regular activities, despite the fact they spent the majority of their savings on attorneys. On top of this, the kids were now shuffling back and forth between two households and she was now functioning as a working single parent, maid, cook, and chauffeur. In her mind, she was just maintaining the lifestyle her friends and neighbors all enjoyed, but she was driving herself further into debt, fueled by anger at her ex. She felt she deserved to maintain her lifestyle. The problem was, her expectations weren't realistic and her behaviors and beliefs were ruled more by emotions than logic. She was adding a ton of stress to her life, but what she really needed was to reflect and simplify.

One of the more difficult things I've had to do in life is let go of unhealthy relationships. I'm a people pleaser by nature, fueled by a need for acceptance that's rooted in my early childhood experiences. But as much as I (or you) may want to keep the people in my life happy, some relationships shift into toxicity and need to be shed or limited. Perhaps you have a friend whose negativity seems unending, who is routinely dishonest or uses others for personal gain. What value does this person add to your life? Now is the time to pull back from relationships that don't nurture you, support you, add value to your life, and cultivate the relationships that do. Not everyone who is unhealthy can be cut out (your spouse's mother is probably here to stay), but think of some boundaries you can introduce to give yourself the space you need to recover and tend to your own needs.

THREE QUESTIONS TO HELP YOU REFLECT AND SIMPLIFY

1. How am I adding stress to my life?
2. Which of my daily habits and routines are healthy, and which are too complicated or stressful?
3. How am I willing to simplify these habits and routines?

Simplification involves cutting back *without feeling guilty.* (Did you get that?) In fact, you should take pride in simplifying your daily routine: you're taking care of yourself. Now is the time to cut back on unnecessary overworking. You may even need to cut back regular work hours if your crisis is significant… *without feeling guilty*. For so many of us, our lives tend to revolve around work, and for some of us, our lives are *defined* by our careers. Yes, life involves work, but it should revolve around things that really matter: relationships, community, love. Yes, you need income. No, you do not need to be thinking about your job twenty hours every day. In the best of times you need to find balance. During a crisis, you need to put self-care and your well-being first.

Let's go back to Nina. In thinking about how she is adding stress to her life, Nina realizes she has put her own medical needs on the back burner to focus on her crisis. Decisions like putting off going to the dentist for her cavity and not seeing her doctor for her follow-up appointment despite her frail health are making matters worse. In evaluating her habits and routines, she realizes mornings are the most chaotic time for the family, and she starts thinking about how she can change them. She also realizes she is focusing on her impending loss rather than preparing herself for the transition that will follow.

Evaluating How We Treat Ourselves

The patients I treat are extraordinarily diverse. I've worked with athletes, artists, parents, students, corporate titans, small business owners. They come to me with an equally varied list of problems: anxiety, depression, hallucinations, drug and alcohol use, bipolar mania, obsessive-compulsive disorder, and countless others. As diverse as they are, one thing many of my patients have in common is the tendency to be harder on themselves than they ever would be on others. At times, I have to put myself in that category alongside them.

Have you ever stopped to listen to your internal self-talk? Have you ever made a simple error and called yourself an idiot? Have you ever told yourself you'll never understand something? You're too fat to wear that outfit? You can't take a day off because it means you're lazy? Too old to fit in? If you are saying things to yourself you would never say to your best friend or to your child, this is your wake-up call. Knock it off. When one of these thoughts pops up, recognize it and stop for a moment, then change it. *I'm not an idiot. I just made a mistake. No biggie. No one at the grocery store, office, or beach cares about my body. Age brings wisdom and a seasoned sense of humor.* And so on.

Let's check in on Nina. In evaluating how she treats herself, Nina realizes she has the tendency to take on everything, become completely overwhelmed, and then rely on her father to bail her out. She begins to reflect on this pattern. She knows she shouldn't have the expectation of being Supermom all the time, but she doesn't know how to change her thinking. She realizes she is going to need some help in this area. She's been relying on her father for so long, she doesn't really know how to rely on herself, and she blames herself for her weaknesses with a constant string of negative thoughts: *I'll never be able to do this alone. I should be better at that. I should be more organized. I don't know why on earth my husband loves me; I just don't deserve it.*

So how does Nina—how do we—change these thought patterns around?

Setting Intentions

My gardener trims the heck out of my avocado tree each spring: it's practically bald when he's finished, and every year, I wonder if he's gone too far. However, he knows there needs to be room for new growth, for new fruit. The sunshine needs to get into the middle of the tree. Cutting back creates the space for healthy growth.

Of everything you've read in this chapter about reflection, simplification, and self-kindness, what resonates with you? Now set your intentions. Evaluate your daily routine and see how it can be simplified. Choose your methods for practicing mindfulness. Maybe you want to try some guided meditations at bedtime to drown out your thoughts. Think about your relationships, what you need, what you can give, and step away from those who don't offer what you want or those who drain your limited resources. In this quiet step of pulling back from the mayhem of a life crisis, ask yourself *What can I do to improve my quality of life on a daily basis?* Then each week, pick one or two to do and give yourself permission to do them guilt-free.

Nina decides she can prep lunches the night before, with her kids' help, to cut back on the arguing and chaos that typically ensue before everyone is out the door for school and work in the morning. She starts lighting candles at the dinner table. She decides to start taking a bath and doing fifteen minutes of gentle yoga and stretching before bed. She decides it will be best for her to cut back on weekend activities and volunteering for the time being to give herself time to unwind or visit with her dad. She also decides to seek therapy to address the long-standing pattern of interaction with her father, with the goal of creating a sense that she *will* be able to move forward after his death. Therapy will also help with her grieving process, and she will learn the techniques she needs to stop her negative self-talk.

The Power of Self-Intimacy

What kind of hippie crap is this? you're wondering. Hear me out. Knowing yourself—taking time to think about who you are and what you value—is empowering. What is important for you in your life? Is it a sense of peace? Then you're going to have to stop fighting with your ex over every nook and cranny in your divorce settlement. (Someone I know spent close to a decade in and out of court fighting with his ex. Trust me, there is *no* sense of peace in that hot mess.) Do you value honesty? Friendship? Loyalty? Humor? Focusing on the things you value instead of the negative circumstances around you promotes healing.

Gratitude is another word that's been hijacked; this time it isn't marketers but therapists who are the culprits. "Start a gratitude journal" has become the elixir for everything. I'm not saying it's without value, but if I hear that phrase one more time, I may actually scream. However, intentionally practicing gratitude has the power to mitigate a crisis.

At its core, gratitude is *acknowledgment and thanksgiving.* How can these be found in a crisis? One way is to look for kindness. Has someone sent a text message checking in with you? Brought over a meal, held open a door? Kindness often goes unrecognized when we aren't looking for it. It's time to start looking.

As Nina ponders what she truly values in life, family bonds and happy relationships are in the forefront of her mind. She decides to work on nurturing a new closeness with her sons and being more gentle (less irritable) with her husband. She decides to adopt the habit of pausing when she finds herself frustrated with them and asking herself, *What is the kind thing to do in this situation?* before responding in words or actions.

Some Final Thoughts About Step Four

Humans function best (and make the best decisions) when we are able to balance logic and emotions. (I often tell patients that if our emotions were always logical, I'd be unemployed.) An exaggerated stress response or a lack of an appropriate stress response are each distress signals. Step Four is about finding that point of balance, so that despite our life crisis, our emotional responses can be appropriate for what is going on *in the moment*, as opposed to being exaggerated by past experiences or by future worries. As you begin your Step Four, be honest in your reflections and kind in how you treat yourself. This is a time to be more scientific than judgmental. In other words, you can reflect through a lens of shame and judgment or use a "scientific approach" that is *more curious than blameful*. Shame and self-judgment lead to isolation and depression. Curiosity creates a space where change becomes possible. Do Step Four with a spirit of curiosity about yourself. And remember, if you're struggling with this and can't see past your own negativity, we encourage you to find a good therapist to discuss these concepts with.

Step Five:
Hold On and Let Go

Kjell Tore

—————————

M Y CLOSE FRIEND JOSEF FACED his life's worst nightmare
when his ex-wife moved their daughter to the other side
of the country on their summer holiday. His daughter was only
a few years old at the time. Josef knew that his ex loved their
daughter very much, so there was no danger to the daughter's
physical safety as far as he could tell—no need to call in the Ma-
rines, just the lawyers . . . maybe. Josef would likely be able to
maintain contact. But still, emotionally, Josef felt his daughter
had been stolen.

Josef confided in me about his emotional status on a daily
basis. The breakup with his ex a year earlier had been painless,
and they had worked well coordinating visitation, school, and
after-school activities over the past year. A psychologist had advised the couple when they split up that it would be best that the
daughter lived primarily with one of the parents so that she
could develop good bonding skills. Josef had agreed to let his

daughter live primarily with her mother. Since the mother was given primary custody, she could move the child on a whim. That's what she did. Now it would be my job as a friend to help Josef survive his life's worst nightmare.

I guided my dear friend through the first four steps of the model: getting a grip, pinpointing what he could control, pushing into motion, and pulling back. Then what?

Before him stood a tortuous journey. Unless I helped my best mate find a sound mental and emotional balance now, he would struggle to function at work, in private, and in his relationship with his daughter in the foreseeable future.

The start of this process of moving forward was for Josef to decide what to cultivate and what to downplay in terms of the person, father, partner, and colleague he wanted to be and to put in place a system to ensure he maintained that balance in his thinking, feelings, and behavior. The term *balance* became our mantra.

Hold On and Let Go

You are the center of your experience; that's where all your thoughts, feelings, and actions originate—not in your partner, not in your parent, not in your child, not in your boss, not anywhere outside of you regardless of the central role these people play in your life. The key to balance is...you! I don't mean this in an egotistical sense of your wishes and self-interests being paramount, but in the knowledge that you are fully responsible for your own thoughts, feelings, and actions—and that's all you can control. So that's where Josef needed to find his balance—in himself. The theme of Step Five—the pinky finger in our model—is thinking balanced, feeling balanced, and acting balanced.

THE TWO ASPECTS TO STEP FIVE

1. *Learn what to cherish and hold on to:* Cultivate the personality traits, characteristics, relationships, and lifestyle choices that you want in your life moving forward.
2. *Let go of the things that don't support your well-being:* Let go of certain thinking patterns, grudges, or personality traits that prevent you from being the person you want to be.

Your Positive Personality Traits

Before there was a crisis in your life and before you were a grown-up pursuing the everyday routines and tasks that grown-ups do, you may have had a season of life when you were young at heart, with infinite possibilities and few responsibilities. What positive qualities do you think of when you reflect on your personality traits, skills, and intellectual abilities from the time of your life with infinite possibilities? It could be anything: humor, curiosity, playfulness, intensity, orderliness, correctness, mischievousness, generosity; the list is as long as humanity is diverse.

Let's look at a sample of positive strengths to inspire you to rediscover strengths from your past that you can cherish and cultivate for the rest of your life. Considerable research has been invested in trying to group people based on clearly identifiable personality traits, without any real success—by this I mean that things are really too complex to fit into neat categories like blood types. But that doesn't mean that the research has been a waste of time. In therapy, terms describing personality traits can be used to help us better understand ourselves and to tweak our self-conceptions so that we can function the way we want to in public and in private.

One of the most commonly used systems to categorize personality traits is called the Big Five (also known as the Five-Factor Model). I'm not suggesting you force yourself to fit into a category, but the model is an interesting starting point for Step Five.

Make a note of one or more personality traits from the ones mentioned above or described below that you feel a kinship to in your current or earlier life. Then think about how bringing it back into focus in your everyday life can help you find your way back to a happier you. Here are some descriptions of close friends of mine who exhibit some Big Five personality traits in order to give you some inspiration.

Agreeableness

My close friend Neil is a good example of the trait of agreeableness. When we are playing an important soccer match with our two teenage sons and a younger child comes over to ask to play with us, he always says *yes*, to the extreme consternation of our sons. They are intent on beating their dads on their own.

Neil is kind, sympathetic, inclusive, warm, and considerate in all things. He treats his partner with the utmost respect and always prioritizes her in the scheme of things. He is faithful to his family and his favorite English soccer team—quite passionate about both—but he knows what to prioritize when push comes to shove. He is modest in his dealings with others, but a solid friend you can rely on when you need a hand.

In my view, one of the most impressive qualities in Neil is the way he treats his "bonus kids"—his wife's children from her first marriage. In every aspect of his daily life, he is able to treat each of the children living in his house equally as individuals with unique needs, strengths, and challenges. One Christmas, when the father of his two bonus kids was going to be alone on Christmas Eve, Neil invited the father to join them for dinner. He made sure that the experience was enjoyable for everyone because he knew how important it was to his bonus kids that their father was not alone on Christmas. I know it took effort on his part, although he would never admit that. His ability to be so inclusive, empathetic and his desire to make any situation easier for those around him exemplifies the trait of agreeableness.

Conscientiousness

My girlfriend in college, Liz, exhibited the personality trait of conscientiousness to a tee. She was organized, efficient, and diligent. When she held parties, she would plan weeks ahead of time. She'd make detailed lists of everything: aperitifs, food, drinks, music, lighting, decoration, entertainment, and backup-plans for possible weather scenarios. (In Norway, we always need a plan A, B, and C to account for weather.) Whatever she set her mind to do, she applied the same systematic, professional approach. I loved this quality about her.

Extroversion

My friend Hedda is one of my favorite people in the world. She is married to a dear friend of mine whom I met when I first started my studies at the University of Oslo. Their house is always full of interesting people, and they are full of stories of all sorts of exciting social encounters.

One summer, when I visited her and her husband, they had a visitor from India staying with them. The visitor was a yogi who had come to Norway to get financing for an orphanage he ran back home in India. Hedda had spent half a year in India taking an anthropology degree and got to know a number of local families. One of these families put the yogi in contact with her. Hedda opened her home to this interesting individual on an important mission for his local community. It was not the first time she had opened her home to people in need of housing. I remember during our student days often entering the kitchen in the house we all shared and finding various international students sleeping on the floor; they had met Hedda out on the town in Oslo, and she would invite them to spend the night in our kitchen.

Anyway, the day I arrived for a visit, the yogi had washed his orange-colored garments and hung them to dry outdoors on the patio. He shouldn't have done that: this is Norway, and Norway is all about weather. When I arrived, pieces of orange-colored clothing had been blown and scattered into every branch and treetop surrounding their house.

It was impossible for us to fish down half of these textiles. Generous as she was, Hedda bought new clothes for the yogi and showed him how to use the washer and dryer in their basement for the next time he needed to wash his clothes. The yogi ended up staying with them all summer. Yet another example of how Hedda's warmth and extroverted personality brought her into contact with an amazing range of interesting people.

Openness

Another close friend of mine, Elin, is a prime example of the trait of openness. In her early twenties, she traveled throughout Asia on her own. Curious and free-spirited, she met other open-minded young people who were eager to explore and learn about alternative ways of living and thinking. Daring to question the straitlaced, conservative, small-town approach to life she grew up with here in Lillehammer, she traveled around the world for a year and a half without any return ticket.

Elin worked a short stint as an English teacher and art teacher at a home for orphaned children in a rural Asian community, where she considered adopting a young handicapped child without parents (but could not get permission as a single woman). Elin combines this trait of being curious and accepting of other cultures, religions, and perspectives with being one of the nicest, gentlest, and most empathetic people I know. She has a smile that can melt a million frowns. Her open personality allows her to see the genius of how other cultures have chosen to organize their lives to make life safe, healthy, and enjoyable for as many as possible. Her openness inspired her to make positive changes in her life that benefited not only her own family but also those of her friends and the local community.

Neuroticism

The only one of the original Big Five personality traits I haven't included here is neuroticism. (I have saved it for the Let Go section later in this chapter.) Although it is the trait that is perhaps best supported in research as being reliably identifiable, it's not a trait you would want to cultivate. In fact, it is closely related to overly expressed emotion, which is exactly what you want to downplay during a debilitating crisis.

THE LIST OF possible positive personality traits is in reality endless, so choose a trait or traits you feel is right for you to cultivate: being gregarious, intellectually curious, easygoing, loyal, faithful, diplomatic, and inspiring. The traits you had in your youth are still in you, so identify them and bring them home.

Your Positive Cognitive Abilities

As a neuropsychologist, much of the work I do on a daily basis involves assessing intellectual abilities such as memory and concentration skills. These types of intellectual skills are referred to as *cognitive abilities*, and they are different from personality traits. When I know a person's cognitive strengths and weaknesses, I can help chart a way forward for the patient at school or work based on his or her strengths while adapting to the patient's difficulties. Take, for example, a young boy who can't sit still in class and has problems remembering his lessons. What is getting in the way of him learning? I want to know if he has impaired attentional focus (a cognitive ability), or if it's just that his mind is full of thoughts about his parents squabbling or bullies lying in wait to hassle him on his way home from school. Giving the kid a pill to boost his concentration won't fix a chaotic home environment or bullying schoolmates.

When I see a person in their fifties who is increasingly losing their keys and forgetting appointments, I have to ask if it is because their memory (a cognitive ability) is getting worse or because they are anxious or depressed.

Just as with the personality traits, the idea here is to identify cognitive strengths in you that will help you move forward in your process of healing and finding balance.

Let's look at a couple of examples of positive cognitive strengths worth cultivating.

Emotional Control

Stopping thoughts and feelings or letting them flow out freely in words or behaviors is a cognitive function that takes place in the front part of your brain. But add into the mix a bubbling cauldron of high-octane emotional fuel generated in another part of the brain and your inhibitory function's ability to play gatekeeper and keep the peace can be overwhelmed.

I have a friend, Anna, who has incredible emotional control. She works as a bartender at a local pub. On any given night, there will be a few fellows who imbibe a bit too much. Anna must deal with rude customers, rowdy revelers, and jerks hitting on her. But no matter what, she is unflappable. At the very least, I would expect her to throw a drink in some guy's face, but she always maintains her cool. If you have this cognitive ability, consider it a strength that will come in handy during any crisis.

Creativity

Another colleague of mine, Elena, is a good example of someone who possesses creativity, which is the ability to see things in a new way, such as making connections between seemingly unrelated things. Elena is a psychologist and amazing at thinking outside the box and playing devil's advocate in situations when everyone else is in agreement. Whenever all of the health professionals are completely in agreement, I always get nervous because it's so easy to overlook something when everyone is looking in the same direction. That is when Elena throws in a torch to make us look more closely at the issue from different perspectives.

When it comes down to it, creativity involves expending the energy to think differently than default mode: default mode is easy and takes less energy. In stressful situations, it is certainly the easy route, but it is not always the best route to take. So applying energy to think creatively when in crisis mode can be an important investment.

Fun, Humor, and Silliness

I don't know of any test in my neuropsychology bag of tricks that can test the fun factor in a person, but I guess most of us know it when we see it: when we do something that brings out the child in us, makes us laugh, makes us not care about how others are judging us (that damned self-conscious loop checking to see that our shirt is tucked in or our lipstick is on right).

It strikes me that very few of the patients I work with on a daily basis have much fun, humor, or silliness in their lives. Their lives are so serious that there is no room for silliness. Being serious all the time is like being stressed all the time—not good for your health. Having fun and being silly relieves stress. A good laugh can work wonders.

I know you may be going through something so terrible that you don't have it in you to even think about fun or humor. And I understand that. It's difficult to smile when your head is spinning and your heart is breaking. However, just try something: sit down and watch a funny movie or television sitcom. Even if you are not initially amused, commit to at least thirty minutes. Allow yourself to laugh. If movies are not your thing, put on your favorite dance music—be it swing, techno, or seventies disco—and get up and dance. Go on. No one is watching. Let yourself feel the rhythm and let your body go. I promise you, you will be smiling before you know it.

Working to put fun back in your life if you don't have it is a healthy approach to reducing stress. I remember reading an article about a famous doctor who after getting a serious cancer diagnosis bought all the funny videos he could find and watched them every day. Not many doctors prescribe Monty Python videos for a cancer diagnosis, but it should be part of their repertoire. The endorphins and dopamine released when you laugh will lighten your mood and relieve your stress. Laughter has also been shown to stimulate your heart and lungs, decrease your blood pressure, and aid muscle relaxation. It seems to me that laughter *is* the best medicine.

Things to Let Go Of

So far, we've discovered strengths to hold on to and cultivate, but the second part of Step Five is to let go of what could be hurting you.

In the "Step One: Get a Grip" chapter, I mentioned that problems that are not faced and dealt with can later surface in the form of psychiatric symptoms. I've seen unresolved issues such as trauma, abuse, infidelity, and humiliation cause physical pain, concentration difficulties, anxiety, depression, anger, and even paranoia. Some of these symptoms can be induced by physical ailments, such as a brain injury or a thought disorder, and others can be self-inflicted from smoking marijuana or the excessive use of alcohol, drugs, and even some medications. The stress itself can also induce these types of symptoms. While serious issues need to be addressed and treated, you can work to let go of things that can be fueling the intensity of psychiatric symptoms.

Earlier in the chapter, I mentioned the Big Five personality trait called neuroticism. This trait is typically defined as having a tendency toward depression, anxiety, anger, insecurity, and perfectionism. These are not characteristics that can be changed easily, but becoming aware of your disposition can help you reduce their impact and adopt strategies to avoid the negative consequences of having these tendencies.

Addressing traits and response tendencies that cause you or other people pain can be an important strategy to improve interpersonal relationships as well. If you can learn strategies to avoid being excessively impulsive, rigid in your thinking, and emotionally insensitive, it will improve the quality of your life and the lives of those around you.

Let's go back to Nina. How did she apply Step Five when working through the model? What did she decide to hold on to and to let go?

Thinking back about her childhood, Nina latched on to her earlier strengths of openness and agreeable personality traits. She brought back into her life a tendency to be positive to new ideas, values, and aesthetics and to be tender-minded to difficult issues, particularly relating to her children, her partner, and her father. She decided she would bring her earlier flexible and creative mindset to find new solutions and favorable outcomes in all her dealings with family members moving forward. She was always strong and knowledgeable in her verbal abilities, and she would seek to use these abilities to communicate more openly and constructively with all of her family members in her daily interactions with them.

She committed to letting go of her pattern of second-guessing herself, doubting her actions, and giving in to pressures to act in ways that were not consistent with her own ideas about how things should be done.

At the same time, she will need to be vigilant of the way in which her father will likely continue to trigger hurtful emotional responses in her that will potentially fuel negative spirals in her thinking. She will identify those thoughts and link them with feelings and events from her past that make sense of her way of reacting. She will use her strength in being kind to herself to acknowledge her intrinsic value, and to love and care for herself in equal measure.

Nina decides to work on temporarily setting aside the many challenges she faces in her daily life and to carve out a time and place to work on becoming more accomplished as an artist. This activity becomes her oasis, and she communicates clearly and straightforwardly to everyone in the family how important it is that they respect her need for this space for herself. Not least of all, she respects this need in herself, at times even ahead of other considerations. This is not egoism; it is finding a balance in her core, which helps her move forward from this crisis.

Moving Forward

Anyone trying to achieve a goal, whether as an athlete, a pupil, a parent, or a good friend, will face hurdles along the way. Expect it. We need to have the confidence to make it through and get help if we need it. And we need to regularly look back while moving forward to think through where we are in the process of working through our crisis. Are we on the right track or not? In some cases, conditions will change, requiring a recalibration of our approach. This looking back as we move forward must be done on a regular basis, depending on the duration of the crisis.

Notice your behavior and your recurring thoughts. Look at your relationships with others and how they are progressing. Are you fighting more? Are you more distant? Do you feel resigned and powerless in your relationship? How you interact with others and how they treat you can offer clues to what's going on with you.

In Nina's case, she is off to a sound start on moving forward on her journey through her crisis, but there are pitfalls ahead. Her father will not likely change his way of communicating despite her being open with him. Even if she does not expect him to change, a subliminal expectation of a change in her father will certainly pose a risk to her emotional state of mind. She will need to practice letting go of negative thought spirals. If she is not able to change the course of her destructive thinking, she will need to get professional help and perhaps even consider medication to help improve her ability to control her thoughts and emotions. She will need to hold on to her healthy daily activities such as sleep, nutritious meals, exercise, and social contact to make sure the basics are in order.

The aim of Step Five is to put you back in the driver's seat of your life. You need to make a conscious choice about what abilities, strengths, relationships, or situations you should hold on to and let go of those traits and characteristics that are not serving you well. Step Five is about moving forward with a balance of strengths that will let you gain a confident stride. Know that you have the ability to regain some control in a situation that seems chaotic.

In an early version of our Five-Step model, we called this fifth step Fly. The idea was that now you had done the hard work of getting a grip on all the layers of a crisis, pinpointing what you can do about it, working through the actions needed to address the problem, and reflecting about your life situation. In this final step, you are consciously emphasizing the traits, abilities, and strengths that have always been who you are to put you in a place for a new beginning—with the faith in yourself to soar!

PART TWO

Applying the Five Steps

AS WE DEMONSTRATE HOW THE steps can be used for various life crises, it is important to keep in mind that the steps don't magically solve the actual crisis itself. The Five Steps don't speed up a grieving process, cure any chronic illness, solve a family or existential crisis, or absolve someone from memories of past traumatic experiences. The work here is about taking a step back and evaluating how the crisis fits into the bigger picture of your life—its meaning in the context of your life experiences—so you can start moving forward despite it. Our past experiences—going all the way back as far as we can remember—in part determine the lens through which we view crises when they occur, and they can leave us focusing on one aspect of the crisis, making it difficult for us to see how much power and control we really have. These steps are about you learning about you, making constructive changes to what you can change, getting help for what is beyond your control, and challenging the feeling of helplessness to a duel.

As you read through the following vignettes, keep in mind that there is no right or wrong here. You may read a story and think you would have done things entirely differently. You will notice how unique these stories and the outcomes are, because the people in the stories are unique, and the therapists (Kjell and I) are also unique, and we sometimes interpret the steps differently despite having created them. The point isn't for you to do what these individuals did in their crises; the point is for you to see the steps applied by people who have been through the stressful crises most of us will (unfortunately) endure in life.

We hope reading these stories gives you confidence in applying the steps to your own crisis and helps you realize you aren't alone in your suffering. Many people suffer through divorce, addiction, abuse, depression, or pain. A crisis is often isolating because our minds are trained to focus inwardly in these situations and it is easy to be caught in negative rumination. While these steps can be worked with someone, they are commonly done alone (or with the guidance of a therapist). While showing how others have worked the Five Steps is meant to encourage you to use them in your crisis, please reach out to someone if you feel overwhelmed, frozen, or overtaken by angst. If you don't have a doctor to guide you, in most areas of the United States you can find a psychiatrist or therapist on the *Psychology Today* website or you can call your insurance company for a list of covered providers. In most of Europe, just contact the local public mental health care provider. You don't have to endure your crisis alone.

Chronic Illness

Depression
Borderline Personality Disorder
Terminal Cancer
Chronic Pain

Depression

Mathias's Story
Kjell Tore

Mathias never liked school, and he dropped out in his teens without completing high school. Now in his mid-thirties, he has been depressed as long as he can remember. For him, it is the normal status quo. After dropping out, he started working to earn money by helping local farmers take care of their animals in the summer and working in the forest in the wintertime harvesting timber. He got his driver's license at eighteen and bought a car as soon as he had earned enough money.

Tall and overweight, Mathias avoids getting into conversations with neighbors or other people in the rural community where he lives, and offers few facial expressions to let people interpret his mood and intentions. To most people, he seems quite serious and stern, and the local kids are scared of him, although he has never been mean to them. To adults who do not know him, he gives the impression of being intellectually challenged. He contacted a local therapist after his girlfriend of a few years, Anita, had threatened to leave him unless he got help for his depressive condition.

Mathias and Anita live together in a mountainous part of the country with a dog and some chickens, far away from the closest city. The only joy Mathias would talk about with his therapist was taking long drives with his girlfriend to go shopping in the city. He felt safe that no one would recognize them that far away. He had been quite a bully in his youth and was afraid of encountering former classmates in his local community whom he had treated badly in earlier times. The past few years, both he and his girlfriend had been smoking marijuana and drinking alcohol when they had the money for it.

Cognitive testing revealed that Mathias had poor verbal understanding and reasoning skills but quite good visual reasoning skills, meaning he was not so good at small talk or long, intellectual discussions, but very good at practical tasks. He tended to be quite impulsive and had a persistent habit of avoiding any challenging task he was asked to do by saying, "You probably think I am stupid."

STEP ONE: GET A GRIP. To start with, Mathias needed to work on gaining some control over his impulsiveness and attentional focus. The neuropsychological testing indicated that his attention span was short, so his therapist would see him in short sessions with a single theme or task per visit. They would start every session with a short breathing exercise, to teach Mathias a strategy to delay impulsive urges. Since his verbal abilities are limited, the therapy sessions needed to be structured in a way that takes advantage of his visual reasoning strengths. Short, practical, motivating tasks can be designed for him to solve in order to help him focus his attention when working through the five steps.

Mathias was able to name a problem he wished to work on to address his depressive mood. The problem he formalized was his lifelong sorrow of feeling like a failure. He hadn't finished high school, and he hadn't been able to hold on to a job for any meaningful period of time. He is currently unemployed. His relationship is strained, and he is certain his girlfriend is about to leave him.

Working through the emotional underpinnings of his feelings of failure, Mathias recognized that he had never had any support in his formative years to achieve any goal or follow through on any challenging activity he wished to pursue. He had developed a recurrent pattern of impulsive interests that he abandoned at the first sign of difficulty. Giving up became a successful strategy for him to avoid failure, and he automatically applied this strategy whenever he sensed problems on the horizon. His parents had struggled with mental health issues as well, and he had been moved into various foster care homes in his early years. He never achieved mastery of any sport, skill, or ability.

The fact that he was tall and strong from an early age, however, gave him physical prowess that he used in his youth to gain a sense of self-confidence. The result as he became older, however, was that it just pushed everyone away from him. Thinking about this now makes him even more depressed as he now understands the anxiety-inducing effect his behavior has had on others.

STEP TWO: PINPOINT WHAT YOU CAN CONTROL

What couldn't Mathias control? Mathias realizes there are many things he has little or no control over. He couldn't control whether or not Anita loves him, if she is faithful to him, or if she ultimately will leave him. Nor could he control the consequences of his earlier bullying. And he is not sure how much his depressive symptoms are the result of a mental condition inherited from his parents, or the result of his difficult upbringing.

What could Mathias control? Thinking through this question, Mathias became aware of many things that he had control over in his everyday life. He could control his daily eating habits, exercise routines, and sleep practices. He does not have any problems falling asleep, but he simply never went to bed until a few hours past midnight. The darkness and stillness of the night seem to calm his fidgety brain. But he could decide to go to bed earlier.

In many areas, he recognized that he could make better decisions for himself to improve his physical and mental health. Moving forward, he can make an effort to treat people fairly and not let his mood and temper get the best of him. Importantly, he recognizes that he can control the way he treats his girlfriend, how he communicates with her, and what activities they can do together to strengthen their relationship. This has become a particular focus for Mathias.

What could he do about the things he couldn't control? Even though he couldn't control his girlfriend's feelings about him, Mathias could control his behavior toward her. He could work to be the best boyfriend he could be. The process would give him self-confidence; the end result is out of his hands. He could be more aware of his tendency to give up quickly, and make an effort to hang in a bit longer when his gut is telling him to give up. And if working through the five steps with a therapist does not relieve his deep symptoms of depression, then he would see a doctor about getting more help.

A serious area of insecurity for Mathias is whether he could actually control his urge to take drugs. He is motivated to stop but realizes that he would have to get help from a specialized mental health professional to control that urge—perhaps having to take medication if needed. He also has the idea to attend couples therapy with his girlfriend to get help communicating better. He realizes that even if he tries to change the way he communicates, many years of misunderstandings might not make it easy for her to understand his new efforts. After all, he is not strong at verbal communication, while that is a strength in Anita. He may have to give her insight into his way of communicating if she is open to learn.

STEP THREE: PUSH INTO MOTION. To start with, Mathias has to find internal motivation to change and work on strategies to get in a more positive frame of mind and practice more constructive behaviors. He is motivated to change, but being positive is unfamiliar territory for him. Yoga and meditation are not his thing, and even the simple act of putting a smile on his face is a challenge. It may take a long time for him to effect change in his way of thinking and to make it automatic. But he can work on his smiles (smiling to people he passes by on his walks) and his comments (complimenting his girlfriend and his neighbors if he dares approach them), to name a few areas of practice.

Mathias divided the specific actions he needs to carry out to counter his depressive mood into Easy Actions and Tough Actions. He made a list of actions he could start working on immediately and actions he would have to work on over time. One thing he can start practicing every morning just before eating breakfast is to take one very deep breath, giving attention to how it fills up his lungs and abdomen, and then follow it up with four long, deep breaths. He also has a list of daily routines he can follow. He recognizes that he will need to ask for help to carry out most of the Tough Actions.

One of his biggest challenges due to his impulsive nature is to learn to apply an internal filter to his thoughts, words, and behaviors when interacting with his girlfriend. An important skill is practicing to delay reacting to emotionally laden comments. When she texts him that she misses him, he will refrain from texting her that he misses their dog. He will stop and take a deep breath—or five—before he responds. In talking with him, the therapist understood that Mathias thought this was funny, but his girlfriend did not see it that way. Working on understanding her perspective will be a long process for Mathias, but it is a necessary step, not only to help the relationship with his girlfriend but also to help him get out of his self-absorbed bubble. The simple process of thinking about how words and actions will affect the person on the receiving end would represent a significant change in his daily interactions with the people in his environment. In particular, his girlfriend.

When it comes to his girlfriend, his focus will not be on "improving the relationship," but on his own actions that will make him a better partner and the habits and behavior that will make his everyday life as healthy and enjoyable as possible.

STEP FOUR: PULL BACK. Mathias realizes that a key prerequisite to establishing a better relationship with Anita is to take better care of himself. The best way Mathias can be kind to himself is for him to stop his habit of criticizing himself for everything he does. He realizes that saying that he is dumb in all contexts in which he is facing a difficult task is an unhealthy defense strategy. He decides to learn new phrases that he can use to build confidence every time he gives his best effort.

Every time he feels the motivation to make changes to his thought and reaction patterns Mathias tends to have a flashback about what a miserable life he has had. All the bad feelings of his past come crashing down on this big man, and it makes him feel like a little boy being smacked down by one of his parents. He decides to take a larger view of his life when this happens. Instead of diving into those feelings of humiliation, he will take a bird's eye view of his life. This will help him see that *then was then* and *now is now*. He does not have control of the "then," but he does have control over the "now."

He has also spent time reflecting on the effect that taking drugs and alcohol had on his ability to control or influence his future in any real way. He has come to understand how his parents lost the war to their own cravings, and he saw how a similar tendency was working to destroy his life and the lives of those close to him. He realizes that he will need help to change some of those destructive behaviors that have become automatic and seemingly impossible for him to control, but he is motivated to choose a future different from the one his parents chose. This new future will be his.

STEP FIVE: HOLD ON AND LET GO. Recalling the traits of his youth, Mathias found that loyalty and an easygoing nature are two qualities from his past that he intends to cultivate. These are qualities he admires, and he sees that they are part of him. He feels they are qualities he can be proud of, and he will use them in his commitment to improve his relationship with his girlfriend. He has gained a belief that every effort he makes toward this goal would give him pride and purpose and affect his mood in a positive direction. He cannot expect these qualities in his girlfriend, but he can commit to exhibiting these qualities in himself in all areas.

He understands the term *loyalty* to mean following through on the promises and agreements he makes. To act on his easygoing nature, he will let go of reacting in an aggressive way when his girlfriend does things that he normally reacts to. Here he will hold on to the new skills of breathing and applying his internal filter to delay his impulsive response pattern. If there are serious issues, such as her taking drugs or alcohol, he can learn to bring them up in conversation in a supportive way. But first and foremost, he can be loyal to his promise to not take drugs himself and in this way be an example for his girlfriend to follow.

Mathias has also always had a fair sense of justice and of what is right and wrong. Even as a young bully, he never preyed on the children who were not able to fend for themselves; he only bullied the children who were unfair to others. At least, this is the way he remembers that part of his life. And if it gives him pride to feel that he can have that role of being on the side of fairness and justice, then this will be an important quality to hold on to in the years ahead. He decides to tap into his strength and sense of fairness to help those in the community less able to fend for themselves when they are treated unfairly.

Mathias decides he will work on letting go of his anger about missed opportunities in his past. He has a chance to work on feeling in control of his life now, so the feelings of loss of control of his life in his past can be placed back in the past where they belong. He also decides to accept his past and let go of his tendency to constantly revisit the shortcomings of his parents. He recognizes that their substance abuse prevented them from being the parents they wanted to be. It's not an excuse, but he decides there is no reason for him to let these feelings hold him back, so he lets them go. He can learn from their mistakes and cultivate a positive attitude of control over his urges to fall into the same trap by instead channeling those urges into positive actions.

Finally, Mathias will need to set up a plan to monitor the progress of his actions on a regular basis with or without his therapist. He has needed help in setting up a program to get him going in the right direction, but in time he will need to put in place his own routines for monitoring how his thoughts, feelings, and behaviors will be aligned with guardrails for him to thrive and grow moving forward.

Borderline Personality Disorder

Melissa's Story
Jennifer

Melissa came to see me after her hospitalization for a suicide attempt. Her boyfriend of four months had suggested they see other people, and she was so distraught that she impulsively ran to the bathroom, locked herself in, and downed several antihistamine tablets. Her boyfriend called 9-1-1; firefighters had to break down the door when she refused to open it, and she was taken to the hospital to have her stomach pumped. She was now going to live with her parents (who made this appointment for her), and they weren't getting along. Melissa felt they were too controlling.

She described difficulty in her life from her early teens. She never felt a true sense of who she was. Her relationships—with her parents, with friends, when dating—in adolescence and adulthood were rocky, tending to vacillate between the extremes of idealized love and fury. She experienced rapid changes in her mood throughout the day, affecting her relationships, work performance (she was usually fired or quit her jobs after a few months), and self-esteem (which she described as "nonexistent"). She tended to live in extremes: things were either great or intolerable. She reported a pattern of impulsive behavior and frequent thoughts of suicide. Melissa initially rejected the idea of therapy, but she agreed to see me for weekly "medication management" visits for one month, and since my shortest medication appointment is thirty minutes, we were able to start discussing the Five Steps at her visits.

STEP ONE: GET A GRIP. Melissa couldn't identify any crisis in her life; she felt her entire life was one big crisis. Everything felt like a five-alarm fire. She identified two escape mechanisms: alcohol and cutting. She would binge on alcohol every weekend, and she noted this worsened her mood and her anxiety the following day. She said she tended to become hypersexual during alcohol blackouts, putting herself in dangerous situations with strangers at bars. When life felt intolerable, she would often cut herself—superficially—to give herself a little physical pain to distract her from her overwhelming emotional pain. Her arms and thighs were covered in scars.

Since her emotions changed so rapidly, I gave Melissa a notebook during sessions to take notes as we went through the steps, "just in case something stood out to her." In our first session, she was able to identify two problems. The first was her fear of abandonment. She realized she was so afraid of this that she would sabotage relationships without intending to. She was pushing other people away before they had the chance to leave her. Then she would feel abandoned anyway and desperately scramble to win back their love. The second problem was her inability to handle stress. She felt so overwhelmed by anxiety that she would often end up feeling detached and numb, unable to process any emotional state at all. This left her feeling disconnected from others and from her own life.

STEP TWO: PINPOINT WHAT YOU CAN CONTROL

What couldn't Melissa control? At her second visit, I asked Melissa what she felt she couldn't control. Her answer? *Anything.* I asked her to name a few examples, and she wrote: mood swings, her behavior when she's drunk, the urge to cut herself, and her suicidal feelings.

What could Melissa control? I asked what she felt she could control. Her initial answer? *Nothing.* She felt everything in life just happened. In fact, she was experiencing an external locus of control.* At that point in time, I didn't challenge her because I wanted her to feel heard.

What could she do about the things she couldn't control? Melissa seemed convinced that nothing could help her, so I asked—theoretically—what might be helpful for someone with mood swings, alcohol binges, and self-injurious behavior? We discussed—theoretically—how therapy can be used to treat mood swings and anxiety, how there were even types of therapy designed to teach coping strategies for high levels of distress, alternatives to self-harm, and ways to address fear of abandonment. I introduced to her the rationale behind a type of therapy called dialectical behavior therapy (DBT) and how it was designed by a therapist with Melissa's very symptoms. She agreed to give it some thought over the week.

STEP THREE: PUSH INTO MOTION. Melissa didn't come to our next session, and I didn't hear from her for several months. When she returned, she said she was tired of being depressed and feeling helpless. Her drinking had caused painful stomach ulcers, and her tension headaches were relentless despite her being under the care of a neurologist and having tried several medications. We discussed how all of this was her own internal motivation making its voice heard, which at first surprised her and then empowered her. After reflecting for a few minutes, she added another motivation: her desire for better connections with people—even though the concept felt completely foreign to her.

We sorted her ideas into Easy Actions and Tough Actions. At first, everything felt tough for her, especially committing to a twelve-week DBT program and giving up her unhealthy coping

---

* You can review external versus internal locus of control in the "Pinpoint What You Can Control" chapter.

strategies of cutting and abusing alcohol. So as an easier task we decided to start working on a "life vision" worksheet together to further help with motivation so she could start to envision what her life might look like once she started learning and implementing the DBT skills. She didn't think she could stop cutting but she thought an easier task would be to call me before looking for something sharp and she volunteered to throw away the scissors she used for cutting. She didn't want to go to Alcoholics Anonymous (AA) meetings or an alcohol treatment program, but her local church had a Celebrate Recovery group she wanted to try out, which was a comfortable, easy task for her. Church was one place she felt accepted.

STEP FOUR: PULL BACK. At her next appointment a month later, Melissa said she "loved and hated" her DBT program. She hated the homework and how some people seemed to dominate the group sessions, but she liked her individual therapist and some of the principles she was learning. She was working through the "self-soothing" section of her DBT workbook, practicing some of her favored techniques when she was stressed. She was also being taught mindfulness and was practicing nonjudgmental observations, which was helping her to regulate her mood swings and decrease her anxiety. She was contemplating pulling back from her dating relationship because she started seeing how unhealthy and abusive it was for her. In our next few sessions, we started to discuss the types of daily routines that seemed to be the most stabilizing for her. She spent time observing what worked for her and what didn't.

STEP FIVE: HOLD ON AND LET GO. Over the course of the next year, Melissa came to see me every other month. After completing her DBT program, she continued in individual therapy so she could have some guidance in applying the skills she had learned to her everyday life. Since she hadn't learned these coping strategies in adolescence, it was helpful to have someone walk her through them in a practical way. Over the year, Melissa was learning to hold on to her new skills and let go of the cutting and self-injurious behavior. She was holding on to her goal of discovering her sense of self in therapy and letting go of hopelessness. She said she may *feel* hopeless, but she no longer had to *believe* she was hopeless or dwell on that feeling when it came. She was practicing holding on to nonjudgmental observations and letting go of harsh self-judgment.

For Melissa, these five steps didn't "cure" her chronic symptoms, and she would find in years to come she would sometimes need to walk through the steps again. Our goal was to improve her quality of life on a daily basis and to manage her condition, not magically make it disappear. Moving forward, Melissa still felt overwhelmed at times, but she decided that when she did she would use one of the self-soothing techniques she loved, grab her workbook, read her life vision worksheet, and start again.

Terminal Cancer

Gretchen's Story
Kjell Tore

Gretchen was called in to see the doctor and given the prognosis: the cancer had spread to her brain. The doctor was direct with her: they could intensify the ongoing chemotherapy immediately, which might slow her disease for a few more months, but this would not stop the spreading, and she could not reasonably expect to live more than six months.

Her husband, Bill, was at home with their five children between the ages of three and seventeen years, waiting for her to return with the news of her prognosis. Bill had wanted to be at the hospital with her when she learned the results of the latest tests, but Gretchen insisted on being informed of the prognosis alone. As a doctor herself, she wanted to be able to ask the questions she needed to know and inquire about possible surgical procedures without the emotional stress of her husband or other family members being present. She had been undergoing treatment for the cancer the past year, and the family was continually hopeful that the chemotherapy would prevent it from spreading. Now the end of her life was certain and foreseeable. More than her fear of dying, the thoughts streaming through Gretchen's head at this moment involved the implications for her family.

Bill had had a more flexible work schedule than her for the past few years and was already doing most of the chores at home and tending to the kids. Gretchen had been working as much as she could to help pay down the mortgage they had on the large house they had just purchased a few years earlier.

On the way home to her family, the normally balanced and harmonious woman was overwhelmed by the challenges that lay ahead. There would be tremendous practical and financial challenges for the family. The oldest daughter was starting college in the next year, and the youngest son had a serious learning disability and social anxiety that required regular attention.

STEP ONE: GET A GRIP. Gretchen had an important decision to make with regard to how to focus her attention going forward. How would she define her problem? She envisaged three alternatives:

1. She could put all her energy in trying to find an alternative treatment—perhaps outside the country—that might help cure her cancer.

2. She could expend her energy grieving over her lost potential and the upcoming turmoil for her family because of this cruel and insidious disease.
3. She could accept the situation and make the best out of the time left for her and her family.

Gretchen thought about the various alternatives. Being the levelheaded person she was, with experience helping others and their families facing similar circumstances, she chose alternative three. Making the best out of a horrible situation would be the problem she would be addressing in her Five Steps. Examining the emotional underpinnings of her problem involved thinking through the history of relationships from her childhood and what words, acts, and events made some relationships more central than others.

Growing up in a relatively poor family in the countryside, it had been a struggle for her to make her way to college and through medical school, but there was always a focus on relationships, with unique bonds developed for each family member. This background would help her focus on what mattered most for her over the next six months.

STEP TWO: PINPOINT WHAT YOU CAN CONTROL

What couldn't Gretchen control? There were plenty of moving parts she couldn't control. Her daily physical and mental energy levels would vary, she would have to follow a treatment schedule her doctors advised, and she may have setbacks and have to be admitted to the hospital for periods of time. Another critical issue that the family did not have control over was their financial situation now that she would not be working as much; the family would be losing her income, on which they had been quite dependent.

What could Gretchen control? Gretchen thought through how she had considerable control over what to do with her time every day for the next six months. Her children would continue their daily schedules as before, but she could adapt her schedule to meet the goals that she set for strengthening the relationships with her husband and each of her children. She was determined that the next six months would be spent cherishing every moment she had together with the people who were most important and needed her presence. From her studies in mental health and her memories from childhood, she understood how the quality of one encounter could be more powerful and memorable than a lifetime of superficial interactions. She could strive to be open for such powerful encounters, not pushing for them or trying to force them, but having the time and the place and the presence of mind for such encounters to touch each of her family members.

What could she do about the things she couldn't control? Gretchen couldn't control her energy levels, but she was intent on taking care of the patients who were depending on her for treatment. She could do what her energy levels would allow and help transition her patients over to other doctors. She could stop taking on new patients, and she could reduce her work schedule to a minimum. To address the loss of income, she could discuss with her husband the pros and cons of making a move to a smaller place rather quickly, so that she could contribute to making the new house a home in the time she had left.

STEP THREE: PUSH INTO MOTION. As never before, Gretchen felt the value of time. During her studies, she had often discussed with her friends what they would do if they only had six months left to live—almost like an exercise in appreciating more intensely the life they had. Earlier, this exercise would generate thoughts of exotic places to visit or outrageously dangerous challenges to accomplish. Now that this situation had become her reality, she realized nothing was as important in her life as strengthening key relationships, and leaving behind as her legacy lessons and memories for her children and husband. This became her motivation.

To begin, she thought of how her mood could influence all her relationships. She may struggle to be positive. She was naturally a very happy, positive individual, but her busy work schedule would often stress her out, and she was often thinking ten steps ahead rather than being in the moment. In addition to becoming aware of her desire to be positive and relaxed in her encounters, she would now be extra aware of being present in the moment with her family members. When her high-school-age son told her about the soccer match he just played, she would see and hear his words and feelings and actions as he experienced them, asking questions about the how and why of the story he was communicating, instead of thinking ahead to prepare a smart comment, lesson, or way forward for his next match. She would be there with him in his thoughts, feelings, and reflections.

Gretchen set up a list of Easy Actions and Tough Actions that would help guide her priorities for the next months. Scheduling and planning time together with each of her family members and writing a to-do list for daily routines were among the Easy Actions she could plan at the start of each week. Perhaps the most important Easy Action was having quality time with her husband. Fortunately, they had a loving and communicative bond, but the power of the situation could cause strains as emotions in both of them were fragile. Among the Tough Actions that she would need help dealing with were the house move, her ongoing medical treatment, and making preparations for her last days. A realtor and her doctor would take charge of the first two Tough Actions. For the third, she allied herself with two close girlfriends who committed to being there for her and the family. It was important for Gretchen that her family continued their normal routines until the end, and with practical help she could focus on the important relationship issues that she felt would give her last days depth and meaning.

STEP FOUR: PULL BACK. Gretchen needed to think of herself in this difficult time as well. She thought about how silly she was with the girlfriends that she grew up with and the crazy things they used to do, and thought about how she might tap into that crazy spirit. Enjoying the simpler, lighter side of life would give everyone in the family a respite from the seriousness of the situation. She started thinking about how she could simplify her life by transitioning out of her job, helping her kids transition into doing more of the chores around the house. She decided massages might help her feel more relaxed around her family, and set the intention to schedule some. She also decided to organize a few weekends away for just her husband and herself.

STEP FIVE: HOLD ON AND LET GO. Gretchen was a popular, intelligent, and successful doctor, wife, and mother with a range of positive traits and characteristics that she could use to reach her goals in the time she had left. She wanted to hold on to her qualities of empathy and excellence in the time ahead, in order to optimize her ability to strengthen meaningful bonds with each of her family members as a caring parent and a role model for her children in their future endeavors.

A more difficult challenge would be to work on letting go of certain difficult feelings that she would struggle with in the months ahead. She decided to stop criticizing herself for not seeking treatment earlier when her symptoms first appeared. As a doctor, she felt that she should have been as vigilant with her own health as she was with others'; however, holding on to such thoughts wasn't adding value to her life, so she decided to let them go.

As part of moving forward, Gretchen agreed with her husband to have a family meeting once a week in which they would discuss the past and coming weeks. This would help give everyone a chance to reflect back and to know what to expect. She had long thought of doing this before she became sick, but they never seemed to have the time and the idea just slipped away. Moving forward, she would put this important platform of communication in place. This would also allow her to have a chance to think back on the goals she had set out for the six remaining months of her life and to gauge if she was on track to achieve the relationship milestones that she had set out for herself and each of her family members.

Chronic Pain

Trevor's Story
Jennifer

Trevor gingerly lowered himself into the chair across from me, wincing stoically. He wasn't sure why he was in my office, other than his parents insisted on it. He knew I specialize in psychiatry and addiction medicine. "I have chronic pain," he told me. "I don't need a shrink, and I don't have an addiction."

In high school, he was a weight lifter and a star wrestler, always the champion in his weight category. He was once thrown down hard on the mat during a match, injuring his back, but he never slowed down his training pace. In college, he was involved in a pretty serious snowboarding accident and was started on pain pills. Over the years, his pain increased, then his medication doses were increased, and soon his pain would increase again. Driving to work one day, he was involved in a car accident, which he felt pushed him over the edge. His back pain was so severe he could no longer work, and he had to move in with his parents. His life became a revolving door of doctors, medication trials, nerve blocks, and steroid injections. His mood became irritable and pessimistic, which he blamed on his pain. He forced himself to go to the gym to maintain his physique, which also caused intense pain, but he felt that was necessary and unavoidable. He told me that some days his pain was so bad that he needed more medication, but his doctors wouldn't prescribe him more, so he was forced to turn to the street, where he was introduced to smoking heroin and fentanyl. All of this, he explained, was the result of his pain, and if his parents would just *understand*, he wouldn't need to be here. It was their fault for not being supportive of his need for more pain pills.

STEP ONE: GET A GRIP. Despite his anger at his parents and externalization of his problems, Trevor acknowledged that he had an increasing dependence on pain medications to manage his mood (resulting in increasing irritability) and that he spent hours playing video games—sometimes up to twelve hours a day and during the night. On the surface, his crisis was threefold: physical pain, increasing use of pain medications and illicit drugs, and failure to launch. Digging deeper, he disclosed something another wrestler said to him in high school that haunted his memory: "You'll never be successful because you're short." He knew this taller student was jealous because Trevor was a better student, a better athlete, and more popular, but nevertheless Trevor held onto the teenager's words deep within his mind, which fueled his escape into video games and increasing use of pain medication after he lost his job. He was trying to escape his fear that this student was right after all.

STEP TWO: PINPOINT WHAT YOU CAN CONTROL

What couldn't Trevor control? His initial answers were: "chronic pain, past injuries, I can't hold a job. I'm disabled."

What could Trevor control? He felt he had some ability to protect himself from future injury and possibly change his attitude. When we discussed his beliefs, he kept repeating: "Doctors can't help me," "Physical therapy doesn't work," and "I can't function without pain meds." He didn't think there was anything he could do about any of that, so we did a little psychoeducation.

PAIN, OPIOIDS, AND FIXED BELIEFS

Chronic pain is tricky. Pain arises from either ongoing dysfunction in a certain area (Trevor's lower back in this case) or from the brain and nervous system replaying an old pain signal that's stuck on a repetitive loop, or perhaps both. At Amen Clinics, we often see overactivity of a brain area called the anterior cingulate gyrus (ACG) in a brain SPECT scan of a person with chronic pain. This part of the brain tends to create rumination and reexperiences of the same things over and over again. We often see the ACG overactive in cases of trauma (when the person has flashbacks to past traumatic events) and in people with obsessive-compulsive disorder (when, for example, the person gets a thought—such as "my hands aren't clean"—and then can't get rid of the thought until she compulsively washes her hands over and over). When the ACG is overactive, we frequently also see overactivity of two areas of the brain (left and right) collectively called the basal ganglia (BG). The BG are supposed to help set the sense of calm for the brain, but their overactivity can lead to anxiety, worry, and anticipating the worst outcome. Additionally, the BG are part of the movement center of the brain, so we see a direct connection between emotional stress and muscle tension. (Have you ever felt shaky before giving a speech or had a relentless eye-muscle twitch during finals week?). Together, these brain areas tend to be associated with overactivity of a third brain area, the deep limbic system, or thalamus. This is part of the emotional center of the brain. So depression, anxiety, and rumination are frequently seen together. You can guess how tough it might be for Trevor to challenge his fixed beliefs (such as *I can't function without pain medication*) because they are rooted in so many brain areas, just like his pain. Having a treatment plan that addresses his pain as well as these brain areas is essential.

Opioids are also tricky. They can be a lifesaver after surgery or a major injury (like a burn) but are really meant for short-term use (other than with certain medical conditions, such as cancer). Longer-term use of opioids starts changing how the nervous system responds to pain, and tolerance develops. This means people typically need to increase their doses over time, creating a nasty cycle: increased pain, increased doses, increased pain, increased doses. The people who come into my office generally have escalated their opioid doses higher and higher over time and have just as much pain—if not more—than when they started them. However, they are terrified of stopping the opioids because they fear even more pain, as well as withdrawal, even while they admit they are miserable.

What could he do about the things he couldn't control? After a little consideration, Trevor decided he could possibly control his thoughts, and we came up with a list of what he could do about the things he can't control. We discussed options of physical therapy or working with an osteopathic physician for osteopathic manipulative therapy, massage therapy, and guided meditations for pain control. He could consider using medication to target his overactive brain areas (the ACG and BG), and he could consider using opioid maintenance therapy (such as buprenorphine) to treat his opioid dependence and bring some stability to his nervous system (and daily life). He could also consider therapy for the emotional trauma his chronic pain has caused and to address his feelings of failure.

STEP THREE: PUSH INTO MOTION. I asked Trevor, "In your worst-case scenario—if you always have some level of pain—do you want to have pain living in your parents' house, unemployed and dependent, or do you want to have pain and have a life?" His motivation for taking action came from shifting his thinking from pain and the mindset of being a "chronic pain patient" to the mindset of life and living. "Since I'm going to *live*, how do I want to live?" I asked him what he thought the hardest parts would be—the Tough Actions. He was terrified of stopping opioids and didn't see the value in letting go of his long-held beliefs that doctors couldn't help him and he'd never get better. I asked what might be easier in comparison—the Easy Actions. He decided dropping the "chronic pain" label wouldn't harm him or be physically difficult, and he could start saying to himself, "Pain doesn't define me." He thought *the idea* of being open-minded wasn't as hard as actually being open-minded, so as an Easy Action he decided to think about these beliefs he created and ask himself whether they were actually true.

While he was working on his Easy Actions, Trevor's pain doctor cut him off after finding out he was seeing multiple doctors for medications, and contacted the other doctors, ending Trevor's legal supply of narcotics. He was forced into Tough Actions. He tried coming off the opioids on his own, but he felt overwhelmed by cravings and withdrawal and ended up using heroin and fentanyl a few times, nearly overdosing. He finally decided opioids couldn't be an option for him and went on opioid maintenance therapy (buprenorphine) to stabilize. He found a good osteopath and started doing osteopathic manipulative therapy and the exercises his doctor gave him.

Importantly, Trevor realized that his thoughts had become "absolutes," holding him stationary in his situation, and he started therapy to work on the Tough Action of challenging his fixed beliefs and developing more flexible thinking.

STEP FOUR: PULL BACK. Once Trevor got into a good rhythm in his action plan, he started to step back and ask himself: *Who am I? What kind of man do I want to be? What do I value?* He realized he always placed a high value on family, which increased his motivation to continue his action plan so he could get into a better position to date and find a partner. He started to realize how video gaming and living with his parents perpetuated rather than alleviated his stress, and he decided he needed some new habits and routines. He decided to study for his real estate license so that once he was feeling better he could start working again. He didn't want to spend his life on disability or unemployed. He focused on meditation for thirty minutes every morning, which he found helped both his mood and his pain, and it also helped him feel grounded in his budding confidence.

STEP FIVE: HOLD ON AND LET GO. Trevor decided to reclaim his old self—the one before the opioids: the funny jokester, the dedicated student, the committed friend. He decided to reclaim his lightheartedness and to start reaching out to old friends. He let go of the old voice of "you're too short to be successful" and decided to hold on to the feeling he had when he was a champion athlete. He would do the same in real estate as he had wrestling. He decided to let go of his identity as a chronic pain patient and to let go of beliefs that don't serve him (such as *I'll never sleep unless I take medication*). This gave him a sense of power over his future and over the outcome of his life.

Moving forward, Trevor was somewhat aware of the high relapse rates and the challenges ahead. He decided to write out some key phrases from his five steps to serve as ongoing motivation. He wrote some on his bathroom mirror; he stuck a note on the dashboard of his car. When he received his one-month-sobriety chip, he put it next to his computer so that when he was studying for his real estate exam he could see this symbol of his new beginning, of his ability to accomplish.

Family Crisis

=====

Addiction
Child with Special Needs
Partner with Cancer
Cognitive Decline
Partner with Traumatic Brain Injury

Addiction

Jeff, Rebecca, Sean, and Shelly's Story
Jennifer

The tension in the house was palpable. Jeff and Rebecca—about to have their twentieth anniversary—were a mess. Neither had slept through the night in months. Jeff was popping antacids every hour, and Rebecca was secretly binging on her hidden stash of sugar cookies in the back of the pantry after their hushed yet heated arguments. She cried so often that she gave up wearing makeup because neighbors and her daughter had frequently pointed out the mascara on her cheeks and she was tired of fielding questions. Jeff spent more and more time away from the house, often leaving before sunrise and returning late at night. He said he was working, but Rebecca didn't know anymore. Part of her didn't even care.

They had been apprehensive when their eighteen-year-old son, Sean, didn't want to go to college but were satisfied with his plan to work at his uncle's roofing company until he figured out his next steps. He worked from 7:30 A.M. until 3:30 P.M., then had the afternoons and evenings to go to the gym, play basketball, and see his friends. Rebecca was a little concerned when Sean started sleeping in a few days a week, but he assured her he was allowed to go in later sometimes. She noticed that Sean had stopped going to the gym and had started looking . . . well, *dirty* all the time, and that his mood became uncharacteristically irritable and oppositional. He said he was working with his hands for a living and she should leave him alone. He would no longer help with the dishes and wouldn't mow the lawn without demanding payment. Then one day, Jeff came home furious: his brother had called, apologizing for having to fire Sean because he hadn't shown up at the worksite more than twice that month. Jeff couldn't believe his brother actually had suggested they drug test Sean! And then reality crashed into his being.

In the coming months, the family struggled. Sean was in and out of the house at all hours of the day and night, appearing disheveled at times, often yelling at his parents. One day while Rebecca was helping their daughter, Shelly, and her classmates with a school project, Sean came home high and passed out on the couch. One of Shelly's friends found him looking blue and screamed, and 9-1-1 was called. This was the first of many overdoses, but the one Shelly remembered the most, because after that none of her friends were allowed to go to her house anymore. Her social life at school came to a standstill. This was when Jeff and Rebecca started arguing—quietly enough, but Shelly heard anyway. And when the fighting ended and her dad stormed out of the house, the tension lingered. Just sixteen, Shelly had no idea what to do.

Jeff and Rebecca were completely split regarding Sean. Rebecca wanted to enforce the "no drugs in this home" policy they had always vocalized. Jeff was afraid to kick Sean out, fearing he would die of an overdose or fall in with an even worse crowd. And so they fought until Sean had his fourth overdose, his fourth trip to the emergency room, and Rebecca put her foot down, telling Jeff this was unfair for Shelly's childhood and unfair for their once-peaceful lives, and if her son was going to die from an overdose, it wasn't going to be in front of their daughter. Upon hearing herself say those words, Rebecca collapsed onto a chair in sobs, and Jeff retreated to his office to research interventions and drug treatment facilities.

STEP ONE: GET A GRIP. Everyone agreed on the elephant in the room: Sean was using drugs and creating chaos for the entire family. Rebecca also identified how the crisis was affecting Shelly's childhood (through the withdrawal of some of Shelly's friends, the fighting in the house), and Rebecca was afraid Shelly might also try drugs because her bond with her brother was always quite strong and she was a curious teenager. Rebecca feared losing Shelly, too. Jeff was terrified Sean would overdose and die. Guided by her parents, Shelly identified that she was scared about Sean, that something might happen to him. Underlying each of their concerns was the realization that the security of their family was in jeopardy.

STEP TWO: PINPOINT WHAT YOU CAN CONTROL

What couldn't anyone control? Sean's behavior and whether he will overdose are both ultimately up to Sean and Sean alone. No one else in the family has control over his choices or behaviors.

What could they control? Rebecca and Jeff agreed they could, theoretically at least, control their household. However, their definitions of control started at opposite ends on the spectrum. Rebecca thought the "no drugs" policy created control, while Jeff thought keeping Sean at home under their watch was control.

They agreed they could schedule time as a family (with Shelly and with Sean, if sober) and they could seek counseling. They could research treatment centers and addiction counselors and offer appointments to Sean. They could schedule time for Shelly—to help with homework, watch her sports, and support her friendships.

What could they do about the things they couldn't control? And what could they do about their vastly differing opinions? Jeff and Rebecca decided they could seek outside help through Al-Anon (and even Alateen for Shelly, if she wanted), family therapy, and/or couples counseling. They could learn how other families have dealt with this type of crisis—what has, and hasn't, worked for them— gathering more information to help in decision-making.

STEP THREE: PUSH INTO MOTION. Rebecca and Jeff each found motivation for action in their hope for Sean. They also wanted to save their marriage, although they knew they were harboring a lot of anger toward one another. They saw a marriage counselor with experience in the field of addiction who helped them first acknowledge the other's position, including how their partner's reasoning was also rational and how there is no one answer that can be applied to every situation. The therapist empowered them, giving guidance with Step Two. Rebecca and Jeff started with the ideas from the therapist they both agreed were good steps—the Easy Actions for them, because they didn't cause any fighting or disagreement. They decided they could remove all alcohol from the house and put all prescription medicine in lock-boxes. They made a list of resources for Sean and, with his permission, put them into his phone in a note: the web page to find local twelve-step meetings; contact information for the local needle exchange, shelter locations, rehabilitation programs, and the Salvation Army treatment program; phone numbers for an addiction counselor and a doctor. They were open to attending some Al-Anon meetings.

It took some time, but they eventually had the energy and strength to tackle the Tough Actions. They decided they could stop supporting Sean's drug use by not giving him any more money, locking away Rebecca's jewelry and Jeff's watch, and keeping an eye on their bank accounts. They were afraid of Sean's response, but felt united in their commitment not to provide Sean resources for purchasing drugs.

At the suggestion of another couple at Al-Anon, Jeff and Rebecca bravely made an appointment with their general practitioner and asked for a prescription for naloxone to have in the house in case Sean overdosed on opioids (his drug of choice now), and they learned how to administer it. They offered Sean an appointment with the doctor, too, so he could get a prescription to have to use for himself or his friends in case of emergency.

They went to counseling sessions weekly and invited Shelly to join them every other week. Sometimes she didn't want to go, and they didn't push her. They offered to go to Alateen with her, and she tried it once or twice. In their family sessions they did the hard work of trying to find mutually agreeable boundaries. For this, their therapist suggested they venture into Step Four.

STEP FOUR: PULL BACK. Because Jeff and Rebecca had different ideas on each of the steps, they committed to trying to understand their tightly held opinions. Upon reflection, Rebecca felt she was being true to herself by holding on to her core parenting rule of "no drugs in this home." She also felt it was her duty to protect Shelly as much as possible from the horrors of Sean's situation.

Jeff felt he was being Sean's protector. Upon reflection, he decided that his authoritarian approach wasn't working and that it was pushing Sean further away. He realized that ultimately no one was winning—or could win—their battle of stubborn versus stubborn. He already knew he was right, but arguing couldn't force Sean to agree.

In therapy, they acknowledged they were completely divided. In one session, their therapist asked them to play it forward: what happens if Sean lives, and what happens if he dies? Either way, both Jeff and Rebecca would use the circumstances to foster their own argument and push the other one away. If Sean lives, it's either "because we gave him boundaries and kicked him out" or "because we let him stay home and we protected him." If Sean were to die, it would be "because you kicked him out" or "because you wouldn't give him any boundaries." The therapist asked them to switch roles in their heads for a week—Jeff would think like a protector of Shelly and Rebecca, and Rebecca would think like the protector of Sean—and they would live in each others' viewpoints for the week. They found it a valuable exercise.

STEP FIVE: HOLD ON AND LET GO. Jeff and Rebecca both held on to Sean by giving him every sober support and resource they could think of. They let go of feeling responsible for his decisions, deciding together in therapy to create a more unified mindset: they would strive to be a positive influence, loving and not blaming themselves—or each other—for Sean's behavior.

They decided to hold on to the idea of family they had before Sean started using drugs. They made time for family activities and date nights. They decided to work on letting go of resentment.

Rebecca decided to hold on to understanding and empathy (for both Sean and Jeff), letting go of negative ruminations on catastrophic "what-if" scenarios. Jeff decided to grasp on to flexible thinking and to let go of "stubbornness for the sake of being stubborn."

Moving forward, Rebecca and Jeff decide to have coffee together outside of the house once a week to touch base on how they think things are going, in addition to maintaining their regular counseling sessions. They will pay attention to whether they are fighting more or less, and what is contributing to it, so they can learn from their experiences. They agree to talk about what brings them closer and what makes them feel distant. They acknowledge their situation can change at any time, which will require each of them to pause for a moment before reacting, and being open to recalibrating their approach to meet the needs of the family.

Child with Special Needs

Patrick, Millie, Dean, and Agnes's Story
Kjell Tore

Agnes just simply refused. She was not going to school that day, not the next day, not ever. She told her parents that if they forced her—as they had done many times earlier—she would jump off the suspension bridge that connected her family's quiet, idyllic island community with the mainland. "I hate you" were the last words the thirteen-year-old said before falling asleep in her mother's arms at 7 A.M. after both had been awake all night.

The day before at school, a boy in her class had noticed that Agnes was doing funny twitching movements with her stomach and had made a point of it in class to the other eighth-grade students when their teacher left the classroom. "Look at Agnes; I think she's going to have a baby," the classmate said aloud to the class, pointing to Agnes's stomach and laughing.

The twitching was something that came and went: at times it was intense, at other times Agnes could control it. Now it was her stomach muscles, at other times she would squint her eyes or squeeze her lips together. She was usually clever at suppressing her twitches during the day at school. The afternoons and evenings at home were another story. Now, with the entire class glaring at her in anticipation, all she felt was her cheeks breaking out into a bright red rash as if a humiliating, deep dark secret had just been exposed to the world and could never be undone. The normally talkative girl was at a total loss for words.

Later that afternoon after school, she would not go out and play with her friends. She said it was because she was afraid of the bees this late in autumn. Yes, she is petrified of bees, but that was not the real reason for her avoiding her friends that day.

Since early childhood, it was normal for Agnes to be up much of the night with little sleep. She would usually start the day exhausted and would struggle to get through the day. Then in the evening, an emotional roller-coaster ride would begin, often at dinner when her parents served something that just rubbed her the wrong way—like food with a sauce that had clumps in it. Other times, it started when her mom followed her to the bathroom to brush her teeth. She would simply refuse to brush her teeth; her heart and thoughts would start racing and nothing could calm her down. Any strong words spoken to her would trigger a volcano of emotion involving foul words, flying objects, and laser-sharp insults hurled with an uncanny precision to exert maximum distress on the nearest family member. A few nights earlier in connection with an unwillingness to brush her teeth before bed, she had called her mother a filthy slut and told her to go drown herself in the river.

After her outbursts, Agnes would often feel crushed thinking about what she had said. These thoughts would be an additional burden weighing down on her budding teenage insecurities. In the heat of the moment, she was not able to control her outbursts. There was one thing Agnes could control, however; she could stop herself from going to school and being humiliated in front of her classmates, ever again.

The urgency of getting Agnes to school had escalated in previous weeks to the point that her parents—Millie and Patrick—were at their wits' end. The school was obligated to report the family to the child protective services agency for their daughter's delinquency, which meant that the family would soon be under investigation. In one meeting with the school nurse, Agnes had been questioned about whether she was experiencing physical or sexual abuse. Agnes's older brother, Dean, had moved out of the house and had gone to live with his grandparents months earlier to get away from the daily drama around his sister. The entire family felt under siege.

Millie and Patrick were firmly committed to facing the situation together. In the heart of this crisis, the committed couple decided to follow the five-step plan together.

STEP ONE: GET A GRIP. The couple started the process by setting aside a weekend to work through the steps and chart out the road ahead. Millie's parents offered to take care of Agnes for the weekend so the couple could travel to a friend's cabin in the mountains. They needed a setting that would give them the space they needed to think and talk freely and to constructively agree on what they needed to focus on in the time ahead.

When they started the process of naming the problem, it turned that out the couple had differing views. Patrick felt the main problem was their daughter missing out on school; Millie felt the main problem was the lack of appropriate therapy for their daughter's emotional outbursts. After discussing their views as well as other alternatives, they agreed that the most pressing problem was for them to ensure their daughter's daily mental well-being and balance—making sure Agnes felt safe, loved, and appreciated every day.

To examine the background for why this issue was of utmost importance, Millie described her experience coming of age—her own experience of being excluded by the "popular girls" as a teenager and teased by the boys about the changes taking place to her developing body. The couple talked about the pressures on youth today and specifically the challenges faced by young girls. Millie talked about the impact these pressures had on her self-confidence, social anxiety, and intellectual development as a young woman.

Patrick admitted that he remembers almost nothing from his youth. All he remembers was that he was a very active boy, passionate about soccer morning, noon, and night, and that his rush to achieve "fame" was supported and driven by his ambitious parents. Thinking back, both thought about how their youth could have been different had their parents parented differently, for good and for bad.

Their daughter's mental and physical well-being became their focus. Making sure Agnes felt good about herself and positive and hopeful about her future every single day was their guiding principle.

STEP TWO: PINPOINT WHAT YOU CAN CONTROL

What couldn't Millie and Patrick control? Millie and Patrick couldn't control their daughter's emotional outbursts, nor could they control her twitches. They also had no control over how the kids at school treated Agnes.

What could Millie and Patrick control? Both agreed that they needed to support each other when Agnes acted out and not undercut each other in the heat of an outburst. They could also control how they interacted with Dean and make sure he had one-on-one time with each of them so that they could meet his needs.

What could they do about the things they couldn't control? Although they couldn't control Agnes's behavior, they could work to avoid triggers and try to regulate their reaction to outbursts when they occurred. They thought about what seemed to work and what did not work to avoid and help defuse escalating emotional trajectories. Although they could not control what happened outside the home, they could spend time talking to Agnes about how other kids can sometimes be mean and suggest creative ways to deal with challenging situations. They could inform teachers, friends, and coaches about her vulnerabilities and how best to deal with incidents.

The professionals at the local child psychiatric services center did not have much experience with the complexity of symptoms Agnes was exhibiting. The parents would have to do the research to find experts who could advise them on how best to treat their daughter's emotional regulation problems. The local and national branches of the organization for their daughter's mental disorder were an important starting point in finding out about therapeutic approaches and available resources. They learned that a therapist trained in Habit Reversal Training techniques could help Agnes gain a measure of control over her involuntary twitches, and they would try to find such a therapist locally.

STEP THREE: PUSH INTO MOTION. To start with, Patrick and Millie addressed the tone of their daily interactions with each other and Agnes. Patrick brought up how he felt that the conflicts with Agnes seemed to become more acute in situations in which they responded with a higher level of emotion than when they were able to stay calm and collected in the face of her meltdowns. Mille in particular would have a tendency to counter Agnes's escalating emotions with frustration and a heightened level of verbal intensity, which seemed to have a provocative influence on Agnes's burning ire. The couple agreed to try to be as positive and nondramatic as possible when Agnes was triggered. Meeting Agnes's flights of emotion with a relaxed and balanced disposition would be an important strategy to decrease tensions. They needed to find a balance of lightheartedness and seriousness. They would have to be able to fill their days with fun and optimism as well, if they were to stay afloat.

In their planning for the road ahead, they divided tasks into tasks that they could do alone (Easy Actions), and tasks they needed to do together or with support from others (Tough Actions). Among the easier tasks were talking to their employers about the need to be flexible in their work situation. They would also have to go to school to inform the teachers and principal of the situation in an open and frank manner. They also needed to discuss how to involve Agnes in these plans and what information she would feel comfortable sharing outside the family.

Several complicated issues would have to be resolved with the help of others outside of the family. They would need support from a psychiatrist to consider possible medication for their daughter, and they would need therapists to help work with their daughter to deal with her emotional control and anxiety issues, and her tics. Agnes's teachers and the school's leadership would have to be involved to help adapt the learning environment to Agnes's needs.

Tough Action would also involve bringing back into the fold an equally important member of the family who had been neglected over the years. Agnes's situation would not get better if she felt guilty that her condition caused her brother to abandon their family. The start of this process would involve each of the parents spending time alone with Dean, with a focus on his interests and activities and gaining his confidence that their love and concern for him was equal to that of his sister.

STEP FOUR: PULL BACK. The parents realized that they had been using Dean as a crutch to help reduce the conflict level at home, without understanding their son's own needs for self-care and self-fulfillment during a critical phase of his emotional, intellectual, and behavioral development. After getting a grip on their situation and working through easy and tough actions, Patrick and Millie paused to consider something they had not thought about before: what about them? In this step, they had to reflect and be creative to find out what Patrick and Millie needed individually and as a couple in the time ahead. They were the foundation on which the family was built, and they needed to carve out space for themselves to keep that platform solid, healthy, and vibrant.

Patrick decided to cut back on his work hours, and they set aside time for each of them to start an activity they had always wanted to pursue. Patrick took a kayak class, and Millie registered to take a Spanish course. They planned date nights and date weekends to show and tell each other about what they had learned. These nights were full of laughter and silliness—serious topics were strictly forbidden. They noticed that when the two of them spent time together as a couple, without the kids, they were more easily able to put things into perspective and view their situation clearly without strong emotions getting in the way. Not only did this help them make important decisions, but it let them step back to recharge so that they had energy for the challenges of their everyday life.

STEP FIVE: HOLD ON AND LET GO. The space Millie and Patrick carved out for themselves in Step Four would help them sustain the love they had for each other. That was the intention, and it seemed to work for them.

Moving forward, Patrick committed to hold on to and cultivate his unique ability to defuse Agnes's emotional responses to triggering situations, and Millie would try to learn these techniques. Millie would hold on to and cultivate her bubbly and expressive personality to create fun diversions and lightheartedness everyday.

Millie also had a unique ability to make everyone in the family feel special and loved, but they agreed that in situations that the couple knew were triggers for Agnes, Patrick would take the lead in calming the situation.

The couple would have to work to temper their frustration with their daughter's health care team. Agnes seemed to follow their lead and developed a negative attitude toward the people who were trying to help her. Instead of being overly critical about everything, Patrick and Millie would view the team they were working with as professionals who were doing the best they could do—just as they were trying to do their best at home with mixed results. Agnes's condition was not common, and they could not expect that everyone working in the mental health field would have good strategies for dealing with this highly challenging mental condition.

Moving forward, Patrick and Millie would need to monitor and evaluate whether all their efforts were showing progress toward an intended outcome or if adjustments had to be made. The journey ahead for Agnes has the potential for pitfalls and problems. She will need a solid bedrock of support at home to help her navigate the path to adulthood.

Partner with Cancer

Tracey and Steve's Story
Jennifer

Time suddenly felt unfamiliar; it was standing still and racing forward all at once, filling Tracey with an eerie sensation. The past few months had been packed with punches: Steve's appointment with his general practitioner for his cough; the confusion when he was sent for an X-ray instead of prescribed antibiotics; the call the following morning requesting that he go to the hospital right way for a chest CT scan; the appointment with the surgeon two days later; the discussion whether to do chemotherapy first and then surgery, or surgery followed by chemotherapy. Steve and Tracey were in their mid-thirties, healthy, getting ready to start their family after settling into their careers. The cough was just bronchitis. It had to be.

After his diagnosis, Steve retreated into his own world, increasing his work projects, spending hours on his laptop wearing headphones. Steve was in a major life crisis, which meant Tracey was, too. She was terrified by the thought of losing him. She wondered whether they would ever have the family they had planned. She was living in fear—joining Steve in sleepless nights and growing fatigue. She saw his stress over his mother's daily calls as he patiently listened to her cry on the phone, openly sharing her inability to deal with her only son's illness. Tracey had no clue how to support Steve. He was about to start chemotherapy, and as positive as he was trying to sound, she could see his stress.

In his own world, Steve didn't want to deal with anything other than his day-to-day survival, so Tracey decided to go through the steps alone. She needed some clarity.

STEP ONE: GET A GRIP. Steve's cancer was unexpected and unfair, and it made Tracey furious. Watching him suffer was horrible, and the feeling of helplessness consumed her. Digging deeper, she realized she had her own crisis going on in parallel to his, but it felt selfish to acknowledge it. With Steve sick, she was now the sole source of income for the family, was now responsible for all of the housework and yard work, and they were accumulating medical debt. She realized she couldn't help but notice the pause in trying to get pregnant; it made perfect sense in their situation, but going back on the pill seemed to take something from Tracey's heart. For years, she had been dreaming of having a family with Steve—picturing what their kids would look like with his ears, her curly hair, his green eyes.

STEP TWO: PINPOINT WHAT YOU CAN CONTROL

What couldn't Tracey control? Steve's health—his lungs, his mood, his sleep, his anxiety, his lethargy, his attitude, his story. She also realized she couldn't control the bursts of emotions she was having, particularly anger regarding her helplessness. She couldn't control her future—what the final financial situation would be after Steve's treatments and whether they would be able to have kids together.

What could Tracey control? Tracey decided she could control her schedule (appointments, work, chores) and her attitude toward it all. She realized she could control her expectations of herself and her thoughts—what she would do with the time she had for thinking.

What could Tracey do about the things she couldn't control? Tracey thought she could contact Steve's oncologist or the American

Cancer Society for resources, education, and support. She could ask about remedies for nausea, low energy, and all the rest of Steve's chemotherapy symptoms. She thought she could maybe do some therapy to talk about her anger and the issues causing her feelings of guilt. She thought she might meet with a financial planner for advice and even talk to Steve about his thoughts on banking some sperm samples before starting chemotherapy.

STEP THREE: PUSH INTO MOTION. With everything going on, Tracey decided to organize and prioritize. She made three categories and put them into the order that resonated with her: Steve, herself, and the house/finances.

For Steve, she called the oncology office and searched the Internet for resources and home remedies, and she made a "chemo kit" for him with ginger chews, his iPad (with his favorite movies downloaded), crackers, a water bottle with a picture of them in their Halloween costumes, tissues, fuzzy socks, peppermints, magazines, Chapstick, and notes from their friends she collected for him to open every day he had chemo. For her, this was as Easy Action.

She decided to make sleep a priority, and she set a sleep schedule for herself, started taking evening walks with her friend every other day, and signed up for a yoga class. These things prepared her for the Tough Task of addressing her anger and guilt. She found a therapist so she could express her fears and emotions and process them with someone other than Steve. She also started doing some simple breathing techniques she learned from her therapist. She met with her human resources department at work to discuss the Family and Medical Leave Act and how much time she would be able to take off when needed.

Tracey changed her expectations for how the yard and house "had" to look. This involved the Tough Action of working on her perfectionist attitude. Although she wasn't confident taking over the finances, she created a budget and set aside a small fund for Steve and her to use to "play" together (they loved going on long drives), and she started saving a little for future medical bills.

STEP FOUR: PULL BACK. Tracey started to mentally prioritize her life, and she found that her two most important priorities were spirituality and her church and her relationships—with her husband, family, and close friends. She realized her career and financial dreams—while important—paled in comparison.

Tracey thought about her mother-in-law's calls to Steve—how much they irritated her because they stressed Steve out so much. She realized how anxious her mother-in-law must be, and she decided to reach out and offer support.

Tracey, her mother-in-law, and even Steve decided to set up a ministry at their church to offer the support and resources Tracey was learning about. She made a list for "chemo kits," lists of tips for getting enough sleep and dealing with nausea and fatigue. The church set up a faith-based support group for patients and/or family members.

Tracey decided to start using her Family and Medical Leave Act days for self-care—yoga, time with her mother-in-law, catching up on the yard, and resting (without feeling guilty).

STEP FIVE: HOLD ON AND LET GO. Tracey decided to hold on to her realization that *all* of her emotions are human and natural and to let go of guilt and self-judgment for them, even if they were negative. She decided to hold on to the current moment: practicing mindfulness, living in the *now*, and letting go of her fear of time passing and her fear of death. She let go of her frustration with her mother-in-law and exchanged it for understanding and compassion for her. She decided to let go of her fantasies and how she wished things could be and to hold on to her belief of life's bigger picture—her belief of what happens when life on Earth ends—and to rely on God's plan for her life.

Cognitive Decline

Greg and His Daughter Amanda's Story
Kjell Tore

The time is never right for developing a serious mental illness. If you make it through the miracle of birth, the screamin' teens, the roaring twenties, and midlife without developing a serious and chronic mental condition, you would think you would have earned a free pass for the rest of the ride. Sadly, the answer is *no*.

Amanda's father, Greg, had suffered a mild stroke that left him with impaired short-term memory, weakened reasoning abilities, and unstable balance. A few months earlier, he had fallen and broken his hip and his right arm.

He had spent his entire life exercising regularly, eating only healthy foods, conscientiously taking vitamins and needed medications, and taking good care of friends, family, and grandkids. His only weakness was an affinity for strongly peated whiskey, but in moderation.

In the blink of an eye, Greg could no longer drive, play golf, find his way around town on foot alone, read and send text messages, or read the fine-print list of ingredients on foods at the grocery store. In conversation, he would talk profusely and his charming personality would convince others that he was just fine, but he struggled to follow the conversation when others asked him questions.

After the stroke, Greg had become more outspoken and less reserved socially, and he frequently talked to strangers he met in parks and at stores. In some ways, this emerging change in personality was like a renaissance for him. He had always been mentally able and fit, but now he spoke his mind at every chance, and if anyone objected he would proudly proclaim, "I don't care what anyone thinks." It wouldn't faze him to tell Amanda which of his girlfriends in his youth had been the best sexual partner. His family members experienced the effect of the stroke as precipitating a change in his personality, but they were unsure if it was a consequence of the stroke or whether the cognitive problems had actually started much earlier. Amanda, who knew him best, felt that things had been getting progressively worse the past two years. Her father had always been a meticulous person, with steely control over his finances, obligations, and attire. Now he increasingly struggled with basic tasks like making breakfast.

Greg had two daughters and one son, but only Amanda was living close enough to help him on a daily basis. She was busy working full-time and shuttling her kids to a wide range of activities, but she called him several times a day and dropped by his house regularly to see how he was doing.

The transition from being in full control over your life to transferring control to others is challenging, and Greg's mental decline was making that process all the more difficult. Amanda felt an overwhelming amount of pressure because she felt that nothing she did was right or good enough. She felt her father needed more help, but he resisted. She chose to work through the five steps to help navigate the way forward for herself and their entire family.

STEP ONE: GET A GRIP. Mental decline in old age varies greatly from individual to individual, depending on a range of genetic and lifestyle factors. Whether changes in those faculties appear suddenly or take place gradually over time, it is important for family members or loved ones to get involved. Amanda had been trying to persuade her father for years to simplify his living situation, without success. Greg insisted on keeping things the same for as long as possible.

Amanda recognized that there were serious issues relating to her father's increasing mental difficulties, physical decline, and increasing need for ongoing support, as well as his ability to manage everything alone. She defined her problem as not knowing how much responsibility to take for her father's well-being.

She also recognized that she was easily triggered by comments that her father would make about her appearance or physical fitness. This had been a recurring issue since her early childhood, and now with every "tut-tut" her father would utter when she took another helping for dinner or an extra scoop of ice cream for dessert, she could feel her temperature rise. Her father had always been the patriarch, making decisions for the family, but now she found herself increasingly in opposition to his views and wishes. This made her feel guilty, but she loved her father and felt she had his best interests at heart. Yet another issue was that her siblings had their own strong opinions about what to do about their father, but they lived far away and were not willing to help in any practical way. The day-to-day demands fell on Amanda's shoulders and she hated that she felt that caring for her father was becoming an emotional burden and a strain on her mental well-being.

STEP TWO: PINPOINT WHAT YOU CAN CONTROL

What couldn't Amanda control? Amanda couldn't control her father insisting that he not move, even if an apartment closer to her home would be more practical. She also had no control over what happened during the day at his house, or what would happen if he were to fall and injure himself while walking to the park or around the neighborhood. In general, she has no control over any degenerative cognitive or biological processes degrading her father's physical or mental abilities, other than to help him keep up a healthy lifestyle.

What could Amanda control? Although Greg refused to live with Amanda and her family, she could call him a few times a day and come over with food and other necessities on a regular basis. Amanda could also encourage her father to have an advance directive drawn up so that there were no questions about his wishes if he were to have an accident and be seriously injured. A will outlining how he wanted his assets divided after his death should be updated as well.

What could Amanda do about the things she couldn't control? What happened with Greg's health was out of Amanda's control, but she could help him follow up with his doctor's appointments. She couldn't force him to move, but she could arrange to have meals delivered daily to her father's house, and get someone to help do the laundry, clean the house, and ensure he was taking his medication. Amanda knows there is a close friend living near her father who could visit him weekly and perhaps take him to the theater or out to lunch so that he has some social interaction with someone his own age.

THREE 3: PUSH INTO MOTION. Amanda loves her father, so there is no question that she wants the best for him. The issue is that she and her father view his best interests differently.

Having gone through the previous steps, the situation became clearer to her. Her father would have to take responsibility for his decisions, and she would take responsibility for hers. He could pay for the help he needed on a daily basis if he decided not to move, and she would make an effort not to become overly involved in his care. His primary doctor could determine if Greg was in his right mind and health to make decisions for himself. As far as Amanda was concerned, she would believe he was until the doctor said otherwise.

Among the Easy Actions for Amanda was making an appointment for her father to visit his primary care doctor. She would also contact a care facility and arrange to have meals delivered daily. Since her father had the financial resources to pay for this help, organizing this service would be easy for her father and the family.

Among the Tough Actions would be getting Greg's physician to make a decision about her father's driving ability. Even though it was clear to Amanda that her father should not drive, Greg refused to give up his driver's license and felt that he would be able to drive after he had recovered from his current balance problems. Amanda insisted that her father's doctor make the final determination.

Another challenging task for Amanda was the call to her siblings informing them of the plan for their father's care. It would be tough because she felt they would judge her for not doing the job herself, but she had made her decision and it was the right decision for her.

Another Tough Action that would have to take place over time was for her to get her father to understand that eventually he would have to move into a care facility, and it would be best to move sooner rather than later. However, Amanda conceded that the final decision about this would be made by her father, unless his doctor strongly felt otherwise.

STEP FOUR: PULL BACK. Amanda recognizes that she also needs to take care of herself in this challenging time. She feels guilty and worried that she will be viewed as selfish by her siblings, but she is confident that this is the correct way forward, also taking into consideration her own family and children's needs.

She is intent on starting a better routine of exercise, sleep, eating well, and avoiding turning to alcohol or food to help her cope with the guilt or pressure. She has good friends to support her and keep her laughing, and she would make a point of spending more time with them.

Amanda also has some health issues that she needs to address. She has been so busy dealing with her father's health issues that she has not been able to get proper treatment for her own. She would hold firm on prioritizing her own health and well-being in the coming months.

In general, she would need to simplify her thinking when it came to her father. As long as possible, he would be making the decisions in his life. Even if he were making risky decisions about his health and spending more money than was necessary, these were his decisions to make. Amanda was determined to not be over-controlling unless her father's physician or other health professional familiar with his mental condition recommended otherwise.

STEP FIVE: HOLD ON AND LET GO. By working through the steps, Amanda became conscious of the need to work actively to cultivate positive traits and characteristics that would help her support her father and preserve her own mental health. She had always been an easygoing individual, and she realizes this flexibility often led to her being taken advantage of and others getting their way. Moving forward, she would be more conscious of communicating clearly her opinion on matters that involved her participation. This would apply not only in relation to care for her father, but also in relation to her other family members. She did not feel the need to force her opinion on anyone, and she was willing to compromise, but she would not be willing to accept decisions made for her any longer. She would put this into practice immediately in regards to her father. It was common for him to make a request and expect her to drop everything to come help him out. Unless it was an emergency, she would now tell him that she would call the care people responsible for his needs and ask them to respond.

Further, going forward Amanda would let go of feeling sole responsibility for obligations that should be shared equally among her siblings.

Amanda would hold on to the innumerable positive memories from the past with her father and the entire family. Greg had played an integral role as grandfather to Amanda's two children when they were younger, and she wanted to focus on these good times.

She would monitor the progress of the medical evaluations led by her father's primary care physician and other specialists working to assess or treat her father's health issues. Greg was the person with the final word for the time being, but he needed Amanda to play that supporting function. She was more than willing to play that role, but it would now be on healthier terms.

Partner with Traumatic Brain Injury

Marjorie and Matt's Story
Kjell Tore

Matt had a passion for mountain biking and traveled around the country whenever he had the chance to compete in amateur events. His twelve-year-old son, Trevor, was also an active mountain biker and his ten-year-old daughter, Ruby, participated in competitions as well. Marjorie didn't enjoy mountain biking as much, and preferred to do other activities, either alone or with their daughter when the boys went biking. Marjorie did accompany the family to competitions as a fervent supporter, though.

When the family was not traveling to participate in races, weekends were spent at their cabin in the mountains, where Matt and the kids often biked on rugged mountain trails in the summer and skied downhill in the winter. The family had a wide network of friends in the neighborhood where they lived and at church. They were blessed with a very active social life.

Matt was a musician and had carved out a niche for himself writing soundtracks for sports-action videos. All his work was done digitally and online, and he had built a studio in his home and cabin where all the magic took place. Marjorie was a nurse at a local hospital. Since Matt's work schedule was more flexible than his wife's, he took a larger share of the parenting respon-sibility for their two kids.

One Saturday morning, Matt and Trevor took a ride in the mountains and made a bet to see who would get down the hill first. The loser would have to buy the winner an ice cream cone. Flying down the course, Matt tried to keep just enough distance behind his son to put pressure on him without overtaking him. At a sharp turn halfway down the course, the ground under Matt's front wheel gave way, causing his weight to be thrust for-ward over the handlebars. With tremendous force, Matt crashed headfirst into a large boulder alongside the trail. He lay motionless.

It took a few minutes for Trevor to realize that his father was not following close behind him. He stopped, then walked back up the hill to find his dad unconscious with blood flowing from his head inside the helmet down onto his racing shirt with the family logo on it.

Horrified and afraid his father was dead, Trevor struggled to find his father's cell phone, and called his mother, who contacted the local air rescue service. Matt was airlifted to the hospital and spent the next six months at a rehabilitation center for traumatic brain injuries. Although the helmet had certainly saved his life, Matt would never be the same. Nor would the family.

The family had health insurance that covered the emergency medical treatment and some of the ongoing care needed to sta-bilize Matt's injuries, but there was nothing in the insurance contract that covered the debilitating mental stress and trauma that Marjorie and their son experienced in the event. The stress would leave deep emotional footprints on their psyches. Not only was there the horror of the accident itself, but Matt had been the key emotional support person for everyone in the family through thick and thin—that was changed forever. Marjorie now had sole responsibility of getting the entire family back on their feet and keeping them there. She needed help to get through this devastating accident, and turned to the five-step model for some scaffolding on her journey through her crisis.

STEP ONE: GET A GRIP. Needless to say, the accident turned the family's situation upside down. The extent of Matt's injuries would remain unclear until Matt regained consciousness, but the doctors had informed Marjorie that the accident had likely caused permanent brain damage, which could lead to lasting behavior and personality changes. She was confident that Matt was receiving the best possible care for his injuries, and realized that she would have to focus on what her changing role in the family would be in the coming weeks and months.

Although Marjorie was devastated at the possibility of losing the love of her life as she knew him, she identified the family's main problem as the immediate need to get the household running without serious disruption for the sake of her children. She was laser focused on putting things in place to reduce the emotional distress for their son and daughter in this critical period of their development. Dealing with her own emotional trauma arising from any other outcome than a full recovery for Matt would take a lifetime to heal and be the occasion for another five-step process.

She went through some of the emotional underpinnings of her fear of being essentially on her own with so much responsibility. First of all, she hated everything to do with finances and had avoided taking responsibility for her money her entire life.

Now she would have to step in and take charge. The fact that she had not been very involved earlier and didn't know much about their financial situation added additional stress to her already overwhelmed mental state.

Another issue was that she had never been as close to Trevor as Matt had been, and she worried how she would be able to take over that role now that she knew Matt may never get back to his old self. A third issue was an extreme anger at Matt for having put himself and their family in such a risky situation in the first place. She had always been afraid of a serious accident, and felt Matt had been selfish to continue mountain biking after they had started a family. They had talked about it several times, and he continued with it and involved the children against her wishes. Now she felt that she had been proven right in her fears, and she was left to pick up the pieces.

STEP TWO: PINPOINT WHAT YOU CAN CONTROL

What couldn't Marjorie control? Marjorie could not control the outcome of the medical treatment Matt was undergoing. Early reports from the doctor indicated he had suffered serious motor impairments, which meant that he would likely need to learn to walk and talk again. The doctors were unsure about the extent of the damage to his overall cognitive abilities, but he would likely not ever be able to work again.

The emotional trauma that their son had experienced was something Marjorie had no control over either; nor over any emotional reactions that her daughter might have. And Marjorie did not have control over how her relationship with Matt would be after the accident. Some of these issues would only become clear in time. Marjorie was completely in the dark about their financial situation as well, since Matt worked freelance and that important source of income was now gone. She didn't even know how much he earned.

What could Marjorie control? Marjorie is able to control the daily routines for the family, such as healthy meals, getting the kids to school, after-school sports and social activities. Most of these things could continue much as before, but now she would have to do the coordinating and driving. She could also ask for help from her family and friends, and communicate her needs clearly to those who could contribute.

What could Marjorie do about the things she couldn't control? Marjorie could get regular updates from the hospital about Matt's condition and communicate any information to her son and daughter in as gentle yet honest way as possible. Visits to Matt will be important to his recovery; he needs to know that his family is supporting him. They will be imortant to the kids too, for they will give them the opportunity to realistically see how their dad is improving.

Marjorie can be supportive of Trevor, who was traumatized by the accident; the horrible images from the day of the crash, and his desperate efforts to rescue his father have been imprinted in his mind. Marjorie can give her son access to a counselor to help him process these emotions, and can open conversations with him too to make sure he is sleeping well and functioning adequately at school.

Marjorie can't control the future of her relationship with her life partner, but for now, she will avoid thinking about how it may or may not be in the future. For the time being, she will stay focused on the day-to-day chores and establishing a realistic financial basis for their future. She can start by getting a solid understanding of their financial situation.

STEP THREE: PUSH INTO MOTION. The difficult situation she is in is all the motivation Marjorie needs to get started on the tasks needed to get the family back on their feet. Her practical disposition and training in keeping a lock on her emotions—during an emergency situation anyway—will help her keep focused on performing the tasks she has set out to do and conscientiously following all the five steps.

Among the Easy Actions for Marjorie will be communicating with her employer to get time off to deal with the family crisis, and communicating with friends and family to get assistance. She can talk to the school and the children's teachers so they are informed and flexible about school schedules should her kids need to be absent from school in the coming months. She will ask them to quickly report any changes they may notice in the children's behavior or performance. Marjorie also decides to contact a close friend of hers who is a financial advisor and can help her get a handle on the family's financial situation. This close friend can also help her make decisions about adapting the family's living arrangements to a future budget.

The Tough Actions for Marjorie are not whether she has to move, or change jobs, or sell possessions such as Matt's car, studio equipment, and/or their cabin. The toughest actions will involve dealing with her children's emotional reaction to the tragic accident and possibly losing the father they once knew, her future relationship with her husband, and the necessary changes in their quality of life, such as less travel, less socializing, and less leisure time. She can try to normalize the situation as much as possible, but she understands that she needs to be ready to ask for professional help when the need arises. And her kids will depend on her being a positive force in their lives.

STEP FOUR: PULL BACK. Trained as a nurse, Marjorie is used to taking care of others and is well-practiced at doing just that. She is not as good at taking care of herself and her own needs. To survive the stress of the stituation and the pressures that would be on her shoulders in the coming months, she would carve out a space just for her that would give her mind and body a rejuvenating break in between the battles.

Part of this process involves her being specific about what she likes to do, what makes her happy, and what makes her heart sing. For ideas, she spends time thinking about fun things she loved to do before she started a family—windsurfing, sailing, bodysurfing and swimming. She grew up close to the beach and is a good swimmer, and being in the water always gave her a feeling of freedom and control. In her youth she often dreamt about being a dolphin dancing through the waves. This image filled her mind and body with happiness. She decides to start swimming a couple of times a week at the local pool, and begins imagining the next family vacation at the beach.

She also remembers having great fun with girlfriends with whom she had lost contact after she started her family. She decides to get in contact with some of these close friends to see if they could reconnect and spend time together.

It is important for her to simplify a situation that feels overwhelming. The big picture is that Matt is in good hands (the doctors), her children are in good hands (hers), and she is on her way to taking good care of herself. She is lucky to have an amazing network of friends and family to support her. Despite the tragic circumstances, this would also be an opportunity for her to develop a closer relationship with each of her children. Thinking about how to do this gives her an exciting and challenging mission moving forward.

STEP FIVE: HOLD ON AND LET GO. Marjorie has always been a dependable, systematic, and levelheaded person. She was the stabilizing force in the family, while Matt was the "sky's-the-limit" force of nature that brought energy and excitement to every corner of their home. She thinks an important first step for her is to cultivate her calm-and-collected approach in order to deal with the difficult time ahead. She needs to provide some stability for her children during this uncertain time.

However, she recognizes that the trauma of the accident weighs heavily on both Trevor and Ruby and she thinks it is important to bring a bit of silliness and fun into the home. She remembers these qualities from the time when she and Matt first started dating—it's what attracted them to each other. She would try to bring back the lighthearted and fun sides of her personality at the appropriate moments in the time ahead.

Among the characteristics she would strive to let go of is her tendency to think and say, "I told you so." She feels an incredible need to scream that out now, but she understands how destructive that is. She decides to work hard on letting go of this feeling of anger. She realizes that Matt was doing something he loved, and with that followed risk. She did not want her reaction to the tragedy to be that she suddenly became overprotective of her children. Of course she wanted to protect them, but she also wanted them to be able to do what they truly loved to do and what truly makes them happy.

Tragedies like this accident can be pivot points that can go in many directions for the family and individual family members. Moving forward, Marjorie will have to assert her presence in her children's lives as never before. She needs to be there for them and bring back a sense of normalcy to their lives.

Loss

================

Divorce
Death of Sibling
Visitation Rights Sabotage
Financial Ruin

Divorce

Lisa and Gary's Story
Kjell Tore

Charismatic and flamboyant, Lisa had been one of the top student athletes in her state, and after four years at an Ivy League college, she became the founder and CEO of a ground-breaking tech firm. She drove in style, lived in style, traveled in style, and partied in style. In thirty minutes, she could transform a boring party of preppy, nerdy guests into a night-of-a-lifetime, in which half the guests swore to quit their jobs, invest all their money in her venture, and dedicate their lives to help her realize her vision. After she left the party, Lisa would never give the encounter a second thought.

Lisa met her husband Gary at an annual consumer electronics show in Las Vegas. Within a few hours of getting to know each other, Lisa had offered him a job in her sales department. Within six months, they were married.

It can be hard to live with a force of nature such as Lisa. Gary was handsome, clever, and artistic, but he had never obtained a level of success anywhere near to Lisa's. His father died when he was very young, and his mother had struggled to raise him and his little brother on meager means. Gary had attended community college but dropped out before earning his degree. He instead got a job in sales working at a local electronics shop.

Life seemed great for the young couple; they lived in a big house in a great neighborhood and entertained often. Lisa quickly got pregnant, and the couple had two kids in less than four years. Gary often talked about going to back to college, but Lisa convinced him that it made more sense for him to be a stay-at-home dad. She made more than enough money, and not working gave Gary time to pursue artistic interests and care for his ailing mom, who was showing early signs of dementia.

As the years passed, Lisa became even more successful. Gary and the kids wanted her to spend more time with them, but Lisa was far too busy with the various business ventures she pursued. She surfed from one triumph to another, but the price was that she spent less time at home and more time at the office and traveling for business meetings. She promised she would take some time off once the businesses could run themselves, but that time never seemed to come. Lisa was riding high on success, and as much as she loved the money, she loved the accolades even more. She was surrounded by followers who admired her brilliance, her creativity, and her magnetic personality. Everyone was in awe of Lisa's golden touch. Everyone except her husband and her kids, who experienced one broken promise after another, one canceled agreement after another.

The day of reckoning came when Lisa returned home from yet another trip to find the house empty. Gary had left a note saying he had taken the kids and was filing for divorce. Lisa pleaded with him to reconsider and promised that she would change her priorities, but Gary had finally had enough. Lisa's money and business acumen couldn't win her the one thing she realized she wanted above everything else—her family.

Their two boys were now preteens and wanted to live with their father. A massive legal conflict was brewing. Lisa started drinking heavily and began suffering bouts of depression. Her closest girlfriends were worried that there was a risk she might even try to take her own life. Lisa's best friend persuaded her to work through the five steps with the help of a therapist. Lisa felt totally lost, but she was a fighter.

STEP ONE: GET A GRIP. This was not the first nor the last time I have seen someone who was smart, talented, and successful run his or her life straight into the ground. I always come back to the same issue: where was that person's attentional focus? More often than not, the focus was exclusively on goals so far and wide that the person lost sight of the near and here. It is admirable to strive for the stars, but without a balanced perspective, you risk losing control and falling hard.

So the start of Lisa's recovery was to find a sound, integrated focus for her future endeavors. Lisa understood that her focus had to be on getting her feet planted firmly on solid ground. Together with her therapist, she formulated her problem as having taken her relationships for granted. Now and in the future, important relationships would be her solid ground.

Thinking through the emotional underpinnings of her unharnassed ambitions, Lisa recognized the ease with which she had mastered most areas in her youth—smartest in her class, best in sports, most popular in school. As a young girl with two older brothers, she was idolized by her family—she was pampered and spoiled and could do no wrong. She was given everything she asked for, and never learned the true meaning of gratitude for what she was given.

Lisa also reflected on her need for constant attention and recognition. It was like a fix that she needed to scaffold her insecurities and hollow self-esteem.

Other issues she identified with the help of her therapist were the impact of her charismatic personality on others and her habit of neglecting the relationships she already had in her search for new and exciting ones.

STEP TWO: PINPOINT WHAT YOU CAN CONTROL

What couldn't Lisa control? She realized that she could not control her ex-husband, who was now happy with a new partner, nor could she control what her children felt about her. She had no control over the looming court case and she was struggling to control her tendency to take a relaxing drink after work and then continuing to drink until she passed out drunk on the sofa.

What could Lisa control? Lisa spent time thinking through what she could actually control in order to start building up her life again. This was a strange, new way of thinking for a person used to believing that she had full control over everything and essentially got whatever she wanted. She was used to working hard to succeed in business but she had never had to work to gain respect in relationships. She had always taken her relationships with her children and her ex for granted, and now those relationships were in tatters. She did, however, have control over how she treated herself and others now and in the future. She had control over her financial situation and how much she worked. She also had full control over what she prioritized in her life.

What could she do about the things she couldn't control? Gary was not going to come back to her, but Lisa needed to have a good relationship with him and his new partner for the sake of her children. Trial or no trial, she had to work to deescalate any conflict so that she could maintain contact with her children. The ball was in her court, because she had the means to make any legal conflict ugly and bitter. The way her children felt about her was out of her direct control, and would be to some extent dependent on her ex's influence on them. However, by straightening out her own life choices and priorities, she had a chance to regain their confidence over time. It was not up to them to change anything; it was up to her to gain their love and respect by her own actions, behaviors, and choices.

She decided that before she could even resume contact with her children, she had to work on getting positive habits, routines, and balance in her life. She would have to get help for her drinking problem, and she would ask for help to treat her bouts of depression. She believed that good routines, healthy meals, exercise, sleep and fun activities and experiences without alcohol would help her depressive symptoms. If these measures didn't help, she would seek professional help.

STEP THREE: PUSH INTO MOTION. Being focused on achieving goals was always one of Lisa's best assets. She knew exactly what to do to charm her way into any secret chamber. But the skills that she could use to win over clients and business associates were not the ones that would win over the people she had let down time and time again. She remembered the saying, *Confidence is lost in buckets and gained in drops.* Her motivation to succeed was sky high, but her current goal line (a repaired relationship with her children) was far into the future. She had to align her behavior with the values that would gain her the love she so desperately longed for.

Lisa went through the process of deciding on Easy Actions and Tough Actions. Among her Easy Actions was a plan to learn how to cook. She had never had to cook anything more complex than a frozen pizza, and she understood that this would be something that she needed to know for when she spent time with her children again, as well as something she could have fun doing together with friends and a future partner. She would also start taking care of her health by making sure to get enough sleep and exercise and find time for relaxation. She would even start meditating to gain better control of her attentional focus. She would also start to reduce the amount of alcohol she consumed during the week to see if she could follow limits she set for herself.

Among the Tough Actions were getting lawyers to help her find a fair agreement with her ex without having to go through a nightmarish legal battle. She would investigate the possibility of getting help at a family therapy center or an arbitration office, to find a balanced and fair outcome. She would work to establish visitations with her children, and she would think through how she could make their time together a positive experience for the kids. This would involve learning about their interests and integrating that into their visits. She knew it would be tough to repair the damage to these relationships, and she would need to be patient to build trust over time and on a solid foundation. She hoped that in time her children would learn to appreciate her positive qualities and see how she was working to improve her life and their relationship.

STEP FOUR: PULL BACK. Lisa realized she had to find her way back to liking herself. Despite appearances of control and command, Lisa had an insecurity issue that was now magnified because so many people had lost confidence in her. Many of the people closest to her—her ex-husband, her children, her siblings, and her former "friends"—viewed her as superficial and someone you could have fun with, but not someone you could trust. Reflecting on this view, she realized that she needed to tone down her strong, impulsive personality and go back to the values of her youth. In the past few years, when she let down friends and they turned her away, she would just move on and find new friends. She realized this was not the way to build solid, long-lasting relationships. She now understood she needed to learn the skill of being a good friend—and she would start with being a good friend to herself.

Lisa realized that in order for others to like her, she had to like herself first. She needed to think about what values she wanted to embrace. She realized that in the past few years she had actually been abusing herself. From now on, she would be kind to herself.

Lisa also reflected on how many things she just never learned to do. She never learned to clean properly (housekeepers did that), make nutritious meals (restaurants handled that), wash her own clothes (a laundry service or her ex took care of that). She had always depended on others to do these things for her, or she would just pay to have them done. She didn't have to be a master chef or an impeccable housekeeper, but she needed be able to take care of herself and her family. Although there were people who admired her for her earlier lifestyle, looking back, she now saw how her life was fake and superficial. These were basic skills she wanted to learn to live a balanced life.

STEP FIVE: HOLD ON AND LET GO. Lisa had many natural talents and skills she could rely on. She decided to hold on to the talents that would allow her to sustain positive relationships over time and not just conquer new superficial ones.

She saw how inconsequential it was for people to be impressed with her success. She would let go of her need of praise and admiration and instead work toward self-validation. She needed to feel good about who she was and what she accomplished. She knew that the process of rebuilding her life from the bottom up would take time and that she needed to be patient with the process. Regularly, she would self-monitor to see how she was progressing so she could make sure any new relationships would be grounded on a sound foundation.

Death of a Sibling

Jason and Elizabeth's Story
Jennifer

The turkey was so heavy, Elizabeth had trouble pulling it from the oven. This was *his* domain: the turkey, the carving, the delivery of the platter to the Thanksgiving table. After their parents had died when they were still in college, she and her twin brother, Jason, had decided they would carry on their family traditions together, and as they married and had families of their own, they had always gathered for the holidays. He took care of the turkey, and she made the side dishes and the pies. The kids always set the table, gathering flowers and twigs from the garden to decorate the table.

The table...where he always sat opposite her, as their parents once sat, presiding over the feast, making everyone laugh with his entertaining stories.

The entire day, as she prepped the stuffing and vegetables, her kids were in the back of her mind. She knew what they were planning in remembrance of her brother. She knew his place would be set, his favorite football jersey hung on his chair. She knew they wanted to remember him on this first holiday without him—retell his old jokes, recall their favorite stories—and she wondered whether she could bear to face that empty chair, that reminder of her loss, of being alone, decades before she should have had to think about it.

In the months since her twin's senseless murder when he had stepped into a fight between a man and his girlfriend on the street, Elizabeth had gone through most of the stages of grief, but she seemed to vacillate between anger and depression, unable to get to the promised "acceptance" everyone talked about. How could she possibly accept *this*?

STEP ONE: GET A GRIP. Since Jason's death, Elizabeth had been living in a fantasy world she was creating in the hours her children were in school. She would pretend grand futures for her brother and herself—future holidays, their kids' graduation parties, their weddings, his retirement party. The days when her fantasies were too difficult to imagine, she turned on the television and watched soap operas, distracting herself with someone else's drama. And meanwhile, the laundry piled up, the house was a mess, meals were disorganized, the kids were late to school and activities, and their homework was often incomplete.

In addition to acknowledging her escape from her grief, getting a grip entailed Elizabeth's discovery that her brother's death reignited old feelings from their parents' deaths, and she realized she actually fears losing everyone she loves and being totally alone. Jason's death was more than the loss of her close twin; it was also the loss of her nuclear family and the person whose presence gave her comfort and stability after losing her parents (which had been her life's biggest crisis up to this point).

Getting a grip would require Elizabeth filling her days with life—not fantasy, not television—and facing her fear of being alone.

STEP TWO: PINPOINT WHAT YOU CAN CONTROL

What couldn't Elizabeth control? She couldn't bring her brother back to life. She couldn't keep trying to make sense of his senseless murder.

What could Elizabeth control? She could control her thoughts, her daily schedule, and her routine.

What could she do about the things she couldn't control? Elizabeth decided she could go to a grief support group while she was dealing with the stages of grief. She thought she might join an aerobics class at the local YMCA, giving her some much-needed exercise, which would in turn help with her sleep and depression and break the monotony of her daytime fantasy and TV life. She also thought she might listen to some guided meditations at bedtime, which was the other time of day that fantasies seemed to take over her mind, leading to stressful dreams.

STEP THREE: PUSH INTO MOTION. Elizabeth acknowledged her anger and realized that her brother's murderer had also taken *her* life and that her children were suffering for it. She created a motivation for herself: "My kids will have the family experience my brother and I had." She categorized her next steps into Easy and Tough Actions. It was relatively easy for her to use her new motivation to start gradually returning to her routine. It gave her the power to turn on music instead of the television, to start planning meals again, make time to do homework with the kids, and clean the house so the family could have a more enjoyable time together in the evenings. She joined an aerobics class and started using a mediation app at bedtime.

The Tough Action for Elizabeth was experiencing grief and making space for her life when she was in the midst of it. She decided to ask her husband and her friend for encouragement in attending a weekly grief support group.

STEP FOUR: PULL BACK. Elizabeth needed to simplify: she just couldn't do all of her household work and typical volunteer work with the exhaustion of her grief. She decided to practice compassion for herself. She didn't want to feel sorry for herself but also didn't want to always be judging her inability to do everything she once did. She decided to nurture herself the way she would nurture her best friend if she was in the same situation. She gave herself permission to say *no* to extra activities for another six months.

In her reflecting, Elizabeth was surprised to realize she was harboring anger at her brother: after all, if he had never intervened in that fight, he wouldn't have been killed. She started the long process of forgiving her brother, forgiving herself for being so angry and "imperfect" (in her eyes), and even forgiving God for allowing it to happen, for allowing her to suffer so much loss in her life.

She took over the family message board in the kitchen, and every night she wrote her husband and each of her children a message, identifying what she appreciated about each of them that day.

STEP FIVE: HOLD ON AND LET GO. Elizabeth decided she needed to tap into the fun-loving humor she once had. She decided to hold on to her memories—to tell stories of her and Jason's childhood and of their parents. She decided to hold on to her friendships and stop pushing people away. She decided to focus not on her loss but on her life—with her husband, kids, sister-in-law. In other words, she let go of her focus on loss in order to hold on to life. Or maybe she held on to life to start letting go of the central role in her life that loss had commanded.

Moving forward, she made the decision to let go of her fears of anticipated future loneliness. She told herself that she isn't alone now, so why does she need to expect it in the future? Every time she had the thought "I'm alone, I don't have family," she would replace that thought with "I have a husband, children, nieces, nephews, and friends who love me and include me . . . thankfully."

Visitation Rights Sabotage

Kirk's Story
Kjell Tore

When Kirk's ex-wife, Kate, moved to the southern part of their state, she moved their two preteen kids with her. She had primary custody of the children, so she had a legal right to move the children against their will—even though neither of the children wanted to move away from where their father was living and where they had grown up. Their mother had been together with a new partner for a couple of years, and he was pressuring her to move or end the relationship. She had brought up her plans with the children, but they were so intensely opposed to moving that she had given up on the attempt at that time. Over the course of the next year, however, she lost her job and felt that she needed a new start. By moving to the southern part of the state, she would be closer to her brother and his family. She eventually steeled herself and made the decision. Kate and her boyfriend purchased a house together without telling the children and didn't let them or Kirk know about their plans until a month before the move.

Kate had promised the children that they would be able to continue with all the sports and activities that they loved in their new home. They were promised that it was an easy drive to visit their father regularly, and they would be starting at a good school. They would also be moving into a much bigger house, so they would each have their own rooms.

Obviously, Kirk was devastated. He had been able to see his kids several times a week as he coached his son's soccer team and his daughter's volleyball team, and they had stayed at his house every other weekend. With the move, he would only see them once a month at best, and possibly for some holidays. He thought about asking if the kids could move in with him, but he knew Kate would never go for that. He could go to court and make a case that staying with him would be best for the children, but would it? His son might want to stay with him, but was it smart to split up the siblings?

Kirk's mind went in all directions. Should he consider moving as well? But what about his job? And his girlfriend? They weren't living together yet, but she was warm and caring, a devoted mother to her own children and a loving partner. Kirk was in love with her and hoped for a future together. Kirk thought his only option was to contest the move and take Kate to court.

That decision didn't turn out well. The fight was ugly, and the children felt like they were being pulled in two directions. The conflict was unbearable to them, and they ended up cutting off contact with Kirk for a period of time and focusing on new friends in their new environment. Kirk felt that his ex-wife undermined his efforts to maintain close contact with their children, and the situation was triggering all types of emotions in him. He experienced the loss of control as humiliating. He realized that it would stay with him for the rest of his life, and he needed to get help to deal with his emotional reactions for the sake of his own mental health and the relationship with his children.

STEP ONE: GET A GRIP. The first order of business for Kirk was to regain his focus on the most important issue that he defined as the problem: maintaining a close relationship with his children. He had always had a very close relationship with both his son and daughter, and they both loved him dearly. A solid focus on this history was an important starting point: there was a solid bond. Emotionally, however, the situation was triggering because of his own experience with his parents. His father had not been part of his life growing up, and his mother had always spoken harshly about his father—how he always put work before his family. Kirk was terrified that this was happening with his own kids now, even though he had always tried hard to be a loving father with the best interests of his children at heart. Even so, he did have a tendency to work too much.

The entire situation brought up issues of trust that he had struggled with earlier in his life. Kate's decision was keeping him from having regular contact with his children, and the crisis had brought up several emotional issues that were important for him to face and resolve.

STEP TWO: PINPOINT WHAT YOU CAN CONTROL

What couldn't Kirk control? The loss of control that Kirk felt stemmed from his lack of contact with his two children. He realized that he did not have control over his kids' feelings for him or his ex's feelings for him. He also couldn't control whether his kids wanted to see him or not, or the outcome of the court case.

What could Kirk control? Although he started from a hopeless feeling of deep loss of control, Kirk realized, when he thought about it, that he did have control over most things in his life. He controlled his meals, his exercise routine, his work performance, his leisure activities, and his holiday trips. He had a strong influence on the quality of his relationships with his girlfriend and his girlfriend's children.

What could he do about the things he couldn't control? Kirk realized he had full control over his words and actions toward his children and his words and actions toward his ex-wife. He needed to choose his words and actions carefully and not let his feelings of humiliation and defeat take control of what he would say and do. As preteens, his kids were not able to decide about visitation issues themselves, but they would be able to in a few years' time. Kirk reasoned that any drama that he might cause in the current situation, despite him feeling it would be justified based on what his ex-wife had done, would not be in the best interest of his children and could possibly cause them to cut him off completely. They would be dragged into a tug-of-war between him and Kate, and no matter who won, they would be the real losers. As preteens, they had other important developmental issues to face without having to deal with a contentious relationship between their parents.

He did need to enter into a concrete visitation agreement so that each visit did not have to be negotiated with his ex, and it would be helpful to get the assistance of a mediator so that the agreement would take into account the needs of all the members of the family.

Importantly, he would take a long-term approach to establishing good contact with his children.

Step Three: Push into Motion. Kirk's motivation came from his decision to focus on a long-term approach to establishing and maintaining good contact and relationships with his children. He worked out a plan for Easy Actions and Tough Actions. He became keenly aware of being positive in all encounters with his ex and his children, realizing that anger and sarcasm would only push him further from his goal. He needed to maintain a connection to his kids, and this would be best ensured by being the happy, loving father he had been before. The contact points with his children might be short, so maintaining positivity during these possibly short conversations on the phone or in person was critical.

Right away, Kirk would get in touch with Kate and request that they work with a mediator. He would regularly call and use FaceTime with the kids, making sure the communication was always light and loving. And he would work to set a date for a future vacation together.

Among the Tough Actions would be figuring out how to make sure he was still involved with the children and their after-school activities. He would have to see if he could have a more flexible work arrangement so that he could take the time off to get to their games and school functions.

Kirk was also intent on seeing a therapist on a regular basis to help him vent his anger and frustrations and to learn strategies and techniques to turn these negative emotions into a positive force for the benefit of his relationship with his kids. Thinking through these plans with an experienced family therapist, possibly together with his girlfriend if she were willing to attend them as well, would be helpful to fulfill his intention of maintaining optimum contact with his kids.

STEP FOUR: PULL BACK. In his quiet moments, Kirk would find himself losing sight of the road ahead and diving into complicated issues relating to his ex-wife, thoughts about what he would miss out on due to not being together with his children, all the things he felt *they* would miss out on, and a range of other thoughts that were making him sad, frustrated, and angry. He decided to rein in his thought patterns, which were only bringing him down. The situation is what it is, and he needed to make the best out of it. By looking at the big picture, he saw that his kids would be moving away from home in a few years anyway, so from a long-term perspective, working on their relationship was key.

An important part of this new reality was for Kirk to be kind to himself. He is a wonderful, loving father despite the situation. He realized he needed to have fun in his everyday life as well and make sure he maintained good relationships with his girlfriend, her children, and his current social network.

STEP FIVE: HOLD ON AND LET GO. Kirk spent time thinking through the personality qualities and characteristics that he wanted to consciously emphasize in the time ahead. He wanted to hold on to being positive, optimistic, social, fun, not overly serious.

He thought these were qualities that his children loved in him and that he would cultivate in his everyday life and when they were visiting. He would hold on to smiles and laughter. It would be a tragedy if this crisis turned him into an angry, sarcastic, grumpy dad.

He would also hold on to his creative skills to plan fun trips and experiences when his children visited. He would plan events for his daughter and son separately and for both children together.

Kirk realized that this crisis had offered him an opportunity to establish even better interactions with his children than before, even though he would see them much less. The crisis had given him a chance to develop a conscious approach to meeting the needs of his children for positive growth experiences moving forward. Even though he had always been committed and dedicated to his children, this was a chance to develop a relationship with them as they developed into young adults that would last a lifetime.

Financial Ruin

Todd and Sally's Story
Jennifer

Todd grew up working on his family's apple orchard on the outskirts of town. He left the farm to study finance at the state college, where he met his wife Sally, who eventually became a teacher. When Todd's parents wanted to retire, he and Sally decided to make a big life change and move their family to the farm to take over the family business. They were shocked to find how mismanaged it had been, but with Todd's financial finesse, they were certain they could turn it around, and they did. They took out a mortgage on the land, Todd planted more trees, and Sally created a roadside farm stand where she sold homemade apple cider and pies. In the fall, they opened a part of the orchard to the public, and soon they became a local attraction for weekend apple-picking trips.

When their college-age son developed a novel app, they decided to invest in his start-up company, channeling much of their profits into the new tech business. Shortly thereafter, some of the neighboring farmers decided to get in on the weekend action, and suddenly Sally had competition for her roadside stand. There were now fresh apple pies on every farm, and the competition annihilated her niche market. Then their son's new company became embroiled in a trademark lawsuit and he lost all of his capital, including their investment. Everything they had worked to build for their future was gone in a matter of months. Todd retreated into his work, rising before dawn and returning to the barn after dinner to tinker around for hours, often not returning until midnight. Sally became so anxious she started waking up during the night in a panic. She was so tense she couldn't work, and she felt she was going through the motions with all of her usual tasks.

STEP ONE: GET A GRIP. Todd felt the pressure of losing the land that had been in his family for three generations. He felt an additional sense of shame because he had majored in finance yet was still in this position. Sally discovered in her internal digging that her anxiety held a familiar quality. She grew up poor and was thrilled to marry someone so stable, but now the old feeling that at any time everything could be taken away returned. She was overwhelmed by the feeling of helplessness from her childhood, when she was powerless to do anything about her family's situation, and she inserted that feeling itself into her present situation.

Todd and Sally decided early on to share their step work together. They discovered how Sally's anxiety worsened the pressure Todd felt, which drove him into the barn to escape, and how his retreating to the barn worsened her anxiety, because she felt more alone. They learned they were playing into each other's weaknesses rather than building each other's strengths.

Step Two: Pinpoint What You Can Control

What couldn't Toddy and Sally control? They decided that they couldn't control their past decisions or the outcome of the lawsuit, and initially Sally felt that she couldn't control her anxiety.

What could Todd and Sally control? They acknowledged that they could control their future decisions. They could control their confidence by going to battle against their automatic negative thoughts. They had control over their schedules, and Sally started to wonder whether she might have some level of control over her anxiety, although she wasn't initially prepared to put it in this category.

What could they do about the things they couldn't control? Todd decided that he would try to shift his mindset from one of shame to curiosity; he would try to learn from their situation. They both realized they would not benefit from replaying the past over and over, and Sally decided she would dive into anxiety management on the Internet and see what she could find.

Step Three: Push into Motion.
Todd's motivation was partly to save face and end his embarrassment, but he also was motivated by his desire to show his son how to overcome failure. He had studied failure in college and knew that all successful entrepreneurs experienced it at some level and used it as motivation, and he wanted to show his son how failure could be motivational fuel rather than glue keeping you stuck in one place. Sally realized she was fueled by fear and resolved to be less anxious. She gave

herself permission to first work on her anxiety level and then go back and work on the business. Beginning with Easy Tasks, they started going on walks together in the orchard after dinner. This gave them both exercise, fresh air, and a renewed love of the orchard and their farming community. The walks helped Sally get out of her head and Todd get out of the barn.

Sally started doing some deep breathing techniques she found online, found the courage to begin her Tough Task, and scheduled some appointments with a therapist who specialized in using cognitive behavior therapy for panic attacks. She went to one session a week for eight weeks and learned some tools for taking back control over her thoughts, which in turn controlled how she felt. Initially, the thought of talking to a therapist about her anxiety gave her *more* anxiety, but she quickly found comfort in the way the therapist was able to understand her, support her, and guide her through her anxious thoughts.

Todd stopped tinkering in the barn so late and got more sleep. His new habits gave him further motivation and energy for his Tough Tasks. He decided to put a few rooms on Airbnb.com, and applied for a license to open a bed-and-breakfast. He approached the neighbors to discuss starting a co-op so they could share the costs and burdens of making the cider and pies as a small community, rather than compete against one another.

STEP FOUR: PULL BACK. For both Sally and Todd, their nightly walks helped them focus on their relationship and family, their history, and the bigger picture. Todd started to evaluate his shame—its origin (self-imposed in early childhood) and the purpose it was "supposed" to serve. He learned to recognize when it was overcoming him and to practice identifying it in the moment and then putting it aside, telling himself that his shame wasn't serving him in this moment and that his mind was going to stay in this moment. Sally also practiced her own version of mindfulness, having recognized that her anxiety was rooted in the past and focused on the future. She decided to gift herself with days when her mind could stay *only* on that day, when she could focus on her tasks that day and not allow her mind to drift to the future or the past, where her anxiety was.

Together, Todd and Sally discussed their long-standing friendships with their neighbors, noting how at some point they seemed to shift from positive relationships to more competitive ones in their own minds. They decided their neighbors didn't intend to drive down their business or harm them, and they reframed their thinking about their friends.

STEP FIVE: HOLD ON AND LET GO. Todd and Sally decided together to hold on to their friendships and let go of resentments; this was easier once they learned to look at intent. If one of them felt wounded, they would ask whether the other person intended to harm them (which is typically not the case in marriage and with friends). If not, they would adopt an attitude of discussion and reconciliation rather than revenge or holding grudges. Sally decided to hold on to her kindness and tap into it more and to let go of thought patterns that only served to promote fear rather than solutions. Todd decided to reclaim his self-confidence and to let go of regrets.

All of this served to power them as individuals and as a couple. It was quite a storm to weather, but easier when they were working together rather than triggering one another. Their marriage strengthened. They had to downsize their lifestyle, trading vacations for more work with the bed-and-breakfast, but they now had the goal of paying off the mortgage and rebuilding their savings. Their midlife crisis became a midlife confirmation in who they were individually and as a couple.

Trauma

Alcoholic Parent
Sexual Abuse
Mass Shooting
Bullying

Abusive Alcoholic Parent

Laura's Story
Jennifer

Laura was forty-eight when she had her first panic attack. She was working at her desk when she was suddenly overcome by the feeling that something awful was about to happen. Her heart started racing; she stood, grabbing her chest, feeling like she couldn't catch her breath. A coworker saw her distress and called 9-1-1. By the time paramedics arrived, Laura was pale, sweating, short of breath, and unable to answer questions, so she was rushed to the emergency room. She had the full workup, was given medication, and began to feel like herself again. A few hours later, when all the results came back negative, the doctor asked her about recent stressors. She couldn't think of a single one, but nevertheless Laura left the ER with a diagnosis of panic attack and a handful of sedatives.

Pretty soon, Laura had another panic attack; this time she knew it wasn't a heart attack, so she took one of the pills the doctor had given her, and within half an hour she was feeling much better. However, these attacks started coming more regularly, at least once a week, always at work, never anywhere else. Laura was perplexed. She also became afraid to go into her office and started using sick days, which she had never before done.

One afternoon, Laura was in her office when her boss's voice bellowed down the hallway once again. He was often yelling at his staff—the coffeepot hadn't been cleaned, the toner in the copy machine was low, the phones weren't being answered fast enough. "This is unacceptable!" she heard him yell, and in that moment she was transported to her childhood bedroom, terrified, as her father screamed in a drunken rage at her mother about Laura's report card. Laura's mother was defending her, her dad was screaming, and she heard the smashing of a plate, the thud of her mother's body being thrown against the wall, and Laura was frozen in place, helpless, praying that he would stop and that her mom would be okay—and that he wouldn't come for her.

She didn't remember much about the rest of that afternoon at work, and oftentimes at work her mind would go blank and she would feel numb and detached, and if she saw her boss in the hallway, she quickly made any excuse to change her direction. She could feel her productivity falling, yet she felt unable to do anything about it and feared her boss's discovery of it. It was just like elementary school: she was unable to focus, afraid of not being good enough, convinced something bad would happen at any time.

STEP ONE: GET A GRIP. The flashback Laura had at work actually started her first step. While she initially thought her problem was the sudden onset of random panic attacks, the flashback made her realize her boss's behavior was actually bringing her back to a time in childhood when similar outbursts meant serious physical harm for her mother or for her. In childhood, her school performance had slipped because of the verbal and physical abuse at home, just as her work performance was slipping now. Even though she logically knew her boss wouldn't physically harm her, her emotions couldn't follow the logic, and the panic that was rooted in her younger self continued.

Digging a little deeper, Laura realized how she had been coping all these years. She worked hard to create a stable, controlled life for herself. She didn't date, she didn't drink, and she honestly felt she was keeping herself safe. She realized, however, that she was isolating from people, withdrawing from having a life, due to her fear of getting close to people. When she was little, she felt so close to her dad . . . and then he hurt her, which left her with very conflicting emotions of both desire for closeness and fear of closeness. Her fear outweighed her desire, so as she grew up, she did everything she could to eliminate the fear, even at the cost of her own happiness. For Laura, not being afraid was good enough.

STEP TWO: PINPOINT WHAT YOU CAN CONTROL

What couldn't Laura control? Laura knew she couldn't control her boss or his behavior at work or the office environment.

What could Laura control? Laura thought she could, in theory, think about whether this job should be her long-term plan or if she should start thinking about possible exit strategies. She could also start thinking about her "controlled" life and safety concerns with relationships, although she didn't know how to get started with any of it. She felt too panicked to think and plan clearly.

What could she do about the things she couldn't control? Laura decided she needed a little distance from her boss to get her panic attacks under control, so she wondered whether she might be able to go on short-term disability for a few weeks until the panic could be treated.

STEP THREE: PUSH INTO MOTION. Laura called a few friends, looked online, and called her primary care physician, and she eventually found a therapist who specialized in treating people who had suffered from abuse and trauma. For her, the research was the Easy Action, and she was motivated by her need to feel less anxious. She also scheduled an appointment with a psychiatrist to discuss options for treating panic attacks other than the sedatives she had been given in the emergency room. She felt out of sorts and a little embarrassed seeing a psychiatrist, but she dug into her motivation and went.

With the support of her therapist and psychiatrist, she decided to take a leave of absence to get out of the triggering environment for four to six weeks so she could do some intensive therapy.

STEP FOUR: PULL BACK. With the help of her therapist, Laura thought about her life, her daily routine, and how controlled she had made it. She always thought she had everything she needed, but now she realized she really did desire connections: she just feared them. She thought about what her life could be—with a few friends, some social activities—without fear in the driver's seat. It was hard to imagine. She was split, both fearing and desiring change. She worked on this in her therapy sessions for several months.

STEP FIVE: HOLD ON AND LET GO. Laura decided to hold on to hope and to continue in therapy to learn how to let go of her fear-driven behavior and life. She decided to hold on to her truth: "I'm missing the good things by spending so much effort trying to prevent bad things." She started to let go of the idea that her childhood experiences defined her. Laura decided to work on letting go of her trauma-based perspective, which is all she had ever known, and to focus on life she could create in the here and now.

Although Laura learned the flashbacks and panic weren't really about her boss' outbursts, she decided to put her feelers out for other positions with potentially less toxic environments and contacted a headhunter. Moving forward, she wanted to make an effort to surround herself with more positive people, and when she hit a trigger she would bring it into therapy to figure out where it was rooted so she didn't have to feel defined or controlled by her anxious experiences.

Sexual Abuse

Julie's Story
Kjell Tore

The police were called to the house in the middle of the night. Julie was high as a kite and was being confronted by her mother, Sylvia, in the basement where she had her room. Julie and her friends were playing loud music and smoking pot, and her mother was trying to kick the friends out of the house. In a struggle to take away a pot pipe Julie was holding in her hand, Sylvia was hit hard on the side of the head and fell to the ground. Friends at the party called for an ambulance, and the police were summoned. Sylvia was taken to the hospital, and Julie was taken to the police station. It was after this that Sylvia arranged for me to work with Julie.

Julie's father had abandoned the family for another woman when Julie was seven. Julie struggled with behavioral problems at school and took medicine for attention problems, but the increasingly larger doses were no longer providing any benefit. Sylvia was struggling to hold two jobs and trying to get Julie to school on a regular basis. She desperately wanted her to complete high school.

A couple of years after her husband left her, Sylvia met Samuel, and they soon married. Sylvia found him to be a stabilizing influence on the family. At the time, Julie was an avid lacrosse player, and Samuel was eager to join Julie at practices, matches, and larger tournaments that often required travel.

Over the past two years, however, Julie had become increasingly aggressive and hostile to both Sylvia and Samuel. Julie's oppositional behavior took its toll on the family. Samuel thought it might be best if Julie went to live with her father.

Julie was barely going to school. She slept during the day and was up all night. Her mother did not know what she was doing at night, but Sylvia suspected Julie was smoking pot with friends. The night before the dramatic episode that led to the confrontation, Julie had told her mother that Samuel had been sexually abusing her the past two years. Sylvia was stunned by her daughter's statement and was in disbelief and denial.

STEP ONE: GET A GRIP. Sometimes a crisis comes after a single major event, but often a debilitating crisis crystalizes after a series of traumatic events. Julie felt everyone close to her had failed to protect her. She was at a crossroads, and it was up to her to decide the path forward: could she put her trust in anyone who could help her to a brighter future or would she be betrayed again? The sexual abuse was true, but she had never told anyone about it. Now that she had, her mother would not believe her.

Julie had always struggled with focusing her attention, so gaining control over her stray thoughts now in her current state of crisis was like trying to herd wild goats. As she started trying to formulate and understand one problem, she would jump to another and then another, and then she would digress and lose her train of thought completely.

To help her along in this process, I explained that she needed to explore one problem at a time for her to gain control over her situation. With some guidance, she was able to name what she felt was her main problem: the severe emotional distress from the abuse was preventing her from making good decisions for herself and her future. Feelings of shame, abandonment, and betrayal made her feel helpless. Thinking through the emotional underpinnings of the problem, however, made her realize that she had never learned good coping skills, and was relying on drugs to escape from the abuse and her feelings about the abuse.

Julie realized that she did have one area in which she had always excelled in making good decisions: playing lacrosse. Since she started playing as a youngster, she always had an instinctive feel for the flow of play. In her mind, she could read developing play patterns better than anyone she knew. The other players used to think of her as a playmaker because of her excellent passes that would help her fellow players score goals. She discovered a resource on which she could build self-confidence. Even though she was no longer on the school team because of her current poor physical condition, she could get back on the team if she straightened out her lifestyle.

STEP TWO: PINPOINT WHAT YOU CAN CONTROL. Thinking through the range of challenges she had to contend with, Julie made a list of things she could control and those that she felt were out of her control, all of which were relevant to her desire to gain trust in her ability to make good decisions for herself.

What couldn't Julie control? Julie had no control over the fact that her father abandoned her when she was seven. She had no control over the sexual abuse that she had been subject to for years as a minor. She had no control over the feelings of betrayal from people close to her, including her mother, who brought an abuser into their household and then didn't believe her when she confided in her. She had no control over her mother's reaction to her hitting her and any legal consequences. Nor did she have control over the concentration and learning difficulties that she had struggled with her entire life.

What could Julie control? Despite the many things that Julie had no control over, she realized that many things were solidly within her control. She could get back in shape so that she could play lacrosse again. She could control her meals, her exercise schedule, and her sleep routines. She could work to get back into good physical condition. She could decide whom to spend time with on the evenings and weekends, and she could decide on the goals she would set for herself over the next years. She was not sure whether she could control her smoking habits, but if she wasn't able to reduce her consumption by 50 percent within a month, she would seek professional help for her dependence.

What could she do about the things she couldn't control? Julie knew there were things in her past she could not change but that weighed heavily on her psyche. She could get long-term therapy to learn how to deal with the feelings of abandonment by her father. She could report the sexual abuse so that the police could investigate and prosecute her stepfather. And she could look into being assessed for her learning difficulties so that if she chose to go back to school the teachers would know exactly what she was struggling with and how to adapt the teaching method to suit her learning style. She could also suggest to her mother that they go together to family therapy to learn to communicate better and establish a trusting relationship.

STEP THREE: PUSH INTO MOTION. To start with, Julie had to find her inner motivation for changing her situation and behaviors, and cultivating a more positive disposition toward herself and her future. She had spent years thinking of herself as a victim, and these thoughts were still on a continuous loop in her head. She had become used to playing the role of victim and had started to use this strategy to avoid making difficult decisions and to excuse her mistakes and failures. She wanted to put that behind her and strive to think and act positively at every turn. The first step would be to start with the person who was closest to her: establishing a better relationship with her mother if she were open for a new start.

Julie made a list of Easy Actions and Tough Actions. Among the Easy Actions that she could start with were apologizing to her mother for any injuries she may have caused her and reaching out to her grandmother and her best friend for support.

Among the Tough Actions were reporting the sexual abuse by her stepfather to the police. As her therapist, I offered to support her in this difficult process, and would report the case to Child Protective Services as mandated by law. I would also refer Julie to a therapist who specialized in treating youth with emotional trauma and to a neuropsychologist for a thorough assessment of her learning difficulties.

STEP FOUR: PULL BACK. Julie took time to reflect on her situation and the changes that she needed to make moving forward. Part of this process was simplifying her life by making daily schedules that would guide her activities toward concrete goals. There was no magic potion for getting back in reasonable physical shape; it simply required a commitment to proper nutrition, exercise, and taking care of her body.

She realized she wasn't taking care of herself or even being kind to herself. No one should go through what she had experienced, and struggling with feelings that the world had let her down had been breeding anger and negative thoughts that she turned on herself. She wanted to work on seeing herself as a good person, a kind person, a valuable member of society, and a person with resources that she could use to help herself and others. She decided to work to sustain kind thoughts about herself, her abilities, and her potential every day.

STEP FIVE: HOLD ON AND LET GO. Julie thought back on the many traits and qualities that had made her so popular in elementary school. She was creative and fearless. She would cultivate these qualities and target them in new, positive directions.

Julie had a lot of anger, which was clearly justified, but this anger was just eating her up inside. She would report the sexual abuse to the police and then let them conduct any needed investigations. It would be out of her hands at that point, and she would have no more control over the process than communicating a true and complete account of the abuse. She decided to let go of the outcome of the investigation, knowing it was out of her hands.

Julie would utilize help from mental health professionals to heal from the abuse, and she also understood that there was plenty she could do herself to heal and move on. She held on to the trust she was building with me and started to rebuild her self-esteem, gradually letting go of her feelings of worthlessness and gaining a feeling of being special and unique in her own right.

Moving forward, Julie would need to integrate positive routines into her life to address the attentional and impulsivity issues she had struggled with since childhood. Julie would learn effective decision-making techniques and strategies from the neuropsychologist she would be referred to, and was motivated to practice them.

Visiting the emotional trauma therapist once a week would help Julie monitor the progress that she had set out for her path to recovery and a brighter future.

Mass Shooting

Chris's Story
Jennifer

While his friends were all swimming and playing volleyball at the beach, Chris was strolling through the appliance store at the local mall, taking advantage of the Memorial Day weekend sale. He decided to walk over to the food court for lunch, and as he got in line to order, a loud *BAM* echoed through the mall. Everyone stopped and looked up, for a moment frozen and confused. Suddenly, they were overwhelmed with the sound of rapid, repetitive *BAMs* echoing around them, and the reality of the situation incited immediate frenzy. People started running everywhere: some fell to the ground under tables, some jumped behind the counter, and then the air was filled with panic as people frantically searched for an exit, a place to hide.

Chris couldn't think—he just ran—until he heard a woman scream for help. She was trying to get her stroller through the sea of now knocked-over tables and chairs, desperately trying to get her young children out of the area. Without hesitating, Chris ran over, picked up the stroller, and started stumbling through the piles of overturned chairs to the edge of the seating area. He was unable to recall much from that day except the sensation that everything around him suddenly slowed down and that he felt detached from everything except for the stroller in his arms and the screams of the mother running beside him— and the moment her screams stopped suddenly.

As the wheel of the stroller caught on an overturned table, Chris felt the stroller suddenly break out of his arms as he fell to the ground. And just as quickly as it started, it was over. Moments of eerie silence froze him in place; no one knew that the shooter had been killed by an off-duty police officer, but the pause in shooting created a mass scrambling of running people.

Chris crawled to the overturned stroller. He heard the child's wails before he got there. The child was bleeding from a cut in his lip, but, thankfully, seemed okay otherwise. Chris turned around and scanned he area for the child's mother. She was laying at an odd angle about ten feet away, a pool of blood beneath her head. Chris didn't have to get any closer to know that she was dead. As days passed, Chris's community was in shock and mourning. Seven people had been killed and a dozen more wounded. His neighbor's teenage daughter had been killed at the coffee shop next to the food court. The sad news just kept rolling in.

Chris was plagued by nightmares and jumped every time he heard a car door slam shut. He couldn't stop hearing the sounds, feeling the chaos, seeing that young mother lying there. He felt guilty that he hadn't been able to protect her, guilty for surviving. He even felt guilty for having so much anxiety; after all, some people had it much worse, so why was he being so weak?

On the Fourth of July, he became unhinged at the sound of the fireworks, spending the entire evening in his closet drinking whiskey. In fact, that soon became a nightly routine to help him sleep and to suppress his horrible feelings for a few hours. It was around this time, when things kept getting worse, that Chris's boss gently suggested he see someone, and his human resources department provided him with a list of therapists.

STEP ONE: GET A GRIP. Chris knew his main issue: the problem was he couldn't forget it. The shooting was itself traumatic, but below the surface, in the aftermath, lived guilt, anger, and loss of control, which kept him feeling terrified. He realized part of his guilt was rooted in his lack of "obvious" wounds. His friends and family kept saying "At least you weren't hurt!" and "Thank

God you're okay!" Chris wanted to yell, "I'm not okay!" He had started to realize a few months prior how hurt he actually was, but he was ashamed to admit it because he survived when so many didn't.

Chris also realized he was using alcohol every night to detach from his anxiety and overthinking, to the point that his boss began to notice. Chris was coming in late, some days hungover, and his productivity was in decline. His boss was being kind, but Chris knew his job would be in jeopardy if he didn't stop drinking.

STEP TWO: PINPOINT WHAT YOU CAN CONTROL

What couldn't Chris control? Chris knew he couldn't have stopped the shooting. He also realized he couldn't stop his symptoms: the nightmares, always being on edge, or his anger.

What could he control? Chris knew, in theory, that he could control his thoughts while he was awake. The only other things he thought he could control were his body and his schedule. This meant he could reconsider his evening routine and think about whether he would continue to use alcohol as his coping strategy every night.

What could he do about the things he couldn't control? Chris thought he could benefit from some grief counseling or support from a therapist because he didn't have a clue how to address his symptoms. He thought about getting involved with gun policy or safety advocacy, but at the time, thinking about it made him feel worse, so he decided to focus first on his recovery.

STEP THREE: PUSH INTO MOTION.
Chris knew that his anxiety was running his life and that his coping strategy (alcohol) was interfering with his happiness and his job. He decided he didn't want the shooter to have any more control over his life, which motivated him to call a therapist. He started learning about the

stages of grief and how common guilt is after a traumatic experience, and his therapist started doing some eye movement desensitization and reprocessing therapy (EMDR) with him, which greatly reduced his reactivity and the triggers to anger and panic. His therapist referred him to a psychiatrist, but this felt like a Tough Action for him, so he decided to try some of this therapist's easier recommendations first. He joined the basketball league at his gym. He started doing a little weight lifting with his teammates, and found the spin class wore him out so much he actually slept more.

With a little sleep and physical activity, Chris felt ready to tackle his Tough Actions. He saw the psychiatrist and learned about options for medically treating his anxiety, nightmares, and the overreactivity of his nervous system.

Chris decided that when he was feeling better he would write to his representative and request resources for getting involved with gun law reform and would look for local nonprofits that advocate in his area. He decided that when he was ready, he would use his voice.

STEP FOUR: PULL BACK. Chris reflected on his daily routine—what was beneficial (the gym) and what wasn't. He took a close look at his social media use, and he decided to "hide" a few contacts who frequently posted about guns and hunting trips and decided to take a break for a few months so he wouldn't have to worry about being triggered by a post, video, or comment. He also stopped watching the news for a few months because it was too triggering.

Chris started to think about what he learned from his therapist regarding post-traumatic guilt. His therapist told him guilt was commonly used as a coping strategy to give a person a sense of control. His self-blame *(If only I had grabbed the mother's hand*

and dragged her along) gave him the sense that if he was ever in that situation again, grabbing more people would change the outcome. In other words, he thought he could have control next time. The downside to this strategy, he learned, was that in reality he couldn't ever control whether someone else would shoot a gun, so this guilt and self-blame were only serving a false purpose and were ruining his self-esteem and daily quality of life.

Chris decided he didn't want to be the guy who drinks every night until he passes out; that lifestyle didn't resonate with his core values, and certainly was making things harder at work and at the gym. He decided he would rather work with the psychiatrist and therapist and throw out the whiskey, and if he was craving it, talk to them about it.

Chris started talking to his friends who—with good intentions—kept telling him, "At least you weren't hurt." He started opening up to a few friends about how hurt he had become that day, and he found most people listened and responded with support and kindness. One friend kept going on rants about gun rights, and Chris decided that since his friend couldn't listen to him with compassion, he would step back from the friendship a bit because it increased his anger and anxiety at this point to engage in those discussions.

STEP FIVE: HOLD ON AND LET GO. Chris decided to let go of the embarrassment and shame and to embrace the process of healing. He held on to truth that he did the best he could under extraordinary circumstances and let go of the guilt that he wasn't shot and the baby's mother was.

Chris let go of his preexisting idea that strength meant not feeling scared and held on to his new definition of strength as being courageous enough to stop escaping, dig deep, and work on getting better.

Bullying

Lenora's Story
Kjell Tore

Lenora was a shy girl who grew up in rural Ohio. Her mother died during Lenora's birth and her father was an alcoholic, so Lenora and her two older brothers mostly had to fend for themselves. Lenora struggled in school. She barely learned to read and write, and she had no patience for math. The other students would make fun of her clothes and her looks, and called her stupid. One day, the teacher scolded her in front of the entire class for not working hard enough at her schoolwork, calling her lazy.

By middle school, she was failing miserably, but her father was either too busy working or drinking to care, so neither did she. The only bright spot in her life was her grandfather. He lived on a small farm in the countryside. Lenora would visit him in the summers, and they would fish and tend his farm animals together. It was the only place and time Lenora felt truly happy. However, her grandfather passed away when she was twelve years old.

At the age of thirteen, she was diagnosed with attention deficit disorder and began taking medication, but she didn't take the medicine regularly, so it wasn't clear if it was helping with her attention problems or not. Every time a teacher complained to her father that she was not working hard enough at school, her father got their doctor to increase her medication dosage.

Because she was so shy and all the boys made fun of her, none of the girls dared to be her friend. She was never invited to parties or sleepovers, although during their lunch break she would hear the girls talk about all the fun they'd had. Being left out was upsetting, but things took a turn for the worse in the seventh grade. Lenora started developing, but in a house full of men, no one talked to her about the changes that were going on with her body. The boys at school teased her mercilessly, but the greatest humiliation came when her teacher sent a note home to her father telling him that his daughter needed to start wearing a bra.

Lenora grew increasingly self-conscious about her body; the way the boys and even some of the male teachers looked at her made her uncomfortable. Without any close girlfriends or family members to talk to about what she was experiencing, she felt alone in the world and struggled on a daily basis to cope with the constant barrage of sexual comments and demeaning looks. She discovered a way to distract herself from this torment: she began cutting herself. She started by cutting the skin on her thigh so it would bleed just a little. It gave her a feeling of control. This became a ritual she would do almost every evening. It was as if the physical pain dulled the mental pain she was experiencing. Then she discovered another form of self-harm that would help her not think about the tremendous amount of stress she was experiencing. She stopped eating. All she could focus on was the hunger pains, so she wasn't able to think of anything else. It gave her a sense of relief and was another way to have some control over her life.

Going to school was torture. She was less and less able to follow the school curriculum and distanced herself even more from the other students. If felt like everyone was staring at her. She became sensitive to anything that was said to her; even well-meaning words from a teacher would be interpreted as sarcasm or an attack. Some of her teachers inevitably stopped interacting with her at all.

By high school, Lenora found a group who welcomed her into their fold. It was a rough group of kids who cut class and drank beer in the parking lot of the local bowling alley. By the time she was sixteen, she dropped out of school and took a job as a cashier at a supermarket. She had no goals, aspirations, or dreams—except to find someone who would be nice to her. By nineteen she was married, and by twenty-one she was divorced.

Now in her forties, Lenora couldn't count the number of sexual partners she has had since high school. One ex-boyfriend introduced her to marijuana and then to more potent substances. She had a preference for painkillers—they dulled her senses. She began to crave them more and more. After one near overdose—she had just wanted to see what would happen if she took a handful—she was referred to a therapist who practiced the five steps. After struggling for years, Lenora felt that this might be her only chance to turn her life around.

STEP ONE: GET A GRIP. Forty-four and without any education or skills, Lenora was feeling lost and abandoned by the world. A childhood of bullying and neglect had trained her in strategies of avoidance and escape, causing her to channel her youthful energy and focus into habits that were self-destructive. She needed to regain her focus—or perhaps obtain it for the very first time—so that she could start building a healthy and fulfilling life for herself.

Together with her therapist, Lenora identified a problem she wanted to work on: her feeling of worthlessness and a lack of self-confidence in her own skills and abilities. Thinking about her childhood, she reflected how her unstable home situation had provided no support for her to develop these important skills, achieve goals, and build a positive self-identity and an emotionally stable foundation. Without any self-confidence, she sought confirmation in her peers and surroundings from an early age. The bullying during her early years imprinted on her a sense of worthlessness. During her teen years, she found a sense of belonging in groups of self-destructive peers who fed on each other's insecurities to build up their own self-worth. She became convinced that self-harm and substance abuse were the only outlets that could give her peace and quiet.

STEP TWO: PINPOINT WHAT YOU CAN CONTROL

What couldn't Lenora control? She felt that the central areas of her life were totally out of her control—particularly her drug use and financial situation. She also couldn't control what others think or say about her. And her past is another area over which she had no control.

What could Lenora control? Lenora thought she could make changes to her daily routines regarding eating, sleeping, and exercising that would provide some balance to her current unstable lifestyle. She also had control over the company she kept, and knew there were friends who pushed her in positive directions and not negative ones.

What could she do about things she couldn't control? Lenora definitely wanted help gaining control over her drug use. She decided she could look for a program or a doctor to help her find ways to free herself from addiction and the destructive self-harm habits she had perfected. She could reach out to her brothers, who, to their credit, had tried in recent years to be a stabilizing force for Lenora. Lenora never graduated high school, but she would like to get her GED, so she planned to work toward that once her life was a little more stable. She would have to apply for financial assistance so she could get back on her feet first. And she could work with her therapist to use the tough lessons from her past to power her drive and commitment to change her life for the better.

STEP THREE: PUSH INTO MOTION. Lenora had avoided eye contact her entire life: it was as if by her looking into the eyes of others, they could see how miserable and sad she felt inside. Looking people

in their eyes had only been possible for her if she took drugs or drank alcohol. Working with the therapist, she found inspiration not to let the bullies in her life control anything about her any more. She was ready to turn the page and move forward with the support and encouragement of her therapist. She was a survivor, and that was something that gave her a sense of strength. Daily, she reminded herself that she was in control of the direction of her life and that each new day was the start of something positive and wonderful for her.

Lenora worked through a list of Easy Actions and Tough Actions. Among the Easy Actions were the daily routines that she would put in place and work on following as best she could. Each day would be structured to provide a balance of sufficient sleep, healthy nutrition, fresh air, exercise, social contact and self-care. She would participate in daily mindfulness sessions online to gain better control over her thoughts and emotions, and spend time thinking about and planning a weekly social activity with a good friend. Among the Tough Actions were areas that she would have to rely on professionals to help her address. She needed help with her drug dependency and would find a treatment program that would give her the tools to work on overcoming her addiction. She would practice the strategies her therapist would teach her on how to deal with impulses to self-harm and overeat, and write a journal documenting her successes in controlling any destructive urges. These processes would take time to learn and master, so an important lesson was for her to be patient with herself and proud of every effort she spent working to change her life around for the better. Perhaps the toughest action of them all was for her to keep alive an inner motivation to succeed in her long-term goal: one day she would get her GED. Her therapist was there for external support whenever she needed a boost along the way.

STEP FOUR: PULL BACK. With her treatment and recovery in motion, Lenora took some time to reflect on her habits that led to her crisis. In her drug treatment program she was learning to take things one day at a time, and because this approach was so helpful, she applied it to the other changes she was making, too. One routine at a time. One activity at a time. One change at a time. She decided to start writing down her daily intentions. She thought she could start by committing to five minutes of reflection and intention every morning or evening, then see if she could increase it over time. She started to write and doodle about positive, concrete things she could do that day. If she felt overwhelmed by negative thoughts, she would write them down and bring them up with her therapist, who could help her work through them.

Lenora decided she wanted to learn how to be kind to herself. She realized she had lived a life of neglect and abuse and had never been taught or shown the value of kindness to herself. She was learning in her therapy and treatment that her first objective was not to *feel* good, which she used to try to achieve by using drugs, alcohol, and food, but to *be* good to herself by engaging in positive and uplifting activities that will bring a deeper sense of satisfaction and happiness. The feelings would follow.

STEP FIVE: HOLD ON AND LET GO. Thinking through the positive traits that Lenora would like to emphasize in the time ahead, she decided that agreeableness is a characteristic that suits her well. She has always been concerned about the well-being of others, and she understands how it is to be treated badly by others.

In terms of positive intellectual qualities, she has always felt one of her strengths is her creativity. She always liked to draw and paint, and she always had good taste in colors, color combinations, and styles. She decided to hold on to her creativity moving forward, and to exercise it by taking up various artistic pursuits.

Lenora's fondest memories are of summers with her grandfather, fishing and tending animals on his farm. She thought
about how she could incorporate these positive memories and
nature in her healing process. She decided she would hold on to
her love of nature. She would begin to take walks in the country
to see and experience scenery that brought back happy, loving
memories of her time together with her grandfather. Perhaps in
the future she could also see if she could volunteer at a local farm.

She decided to let go of self-defeating beliefs that had come
to her mind so automatically when she first started treatment.
She let go of her belief that her only escape from emotional pain
is physical pain or substance abuse. She let go of her belief that
she was all the terrible things her classmates said she was.

At times, Lenora would experience a longing for the familiar
feelings of her previous life of self-harm, physical abuse, and
drugs. She realized this would require frequent monitoring to
ensure she was on her chosen path going forward. Just as she
became emotionally attached to her earlier destructive life, she
also can learn to attach to the idea that she can create a beautiful
and fulfilling life ahead. She dusted off happy memories from
her past and linked them to current joyful experiences that she
can use to support her emotionally in her healing process. It will
require a lifelong monitoring of direction, course, and goals, but
she finally feels worthy of building a quality future for herself.

Existential Crisis

Midlife Affair
Suicide
Chronic Worry
Spiritual Crisis

Midlife Affair

Maggie's Story
Kjell Tore

The telephone rang. It was Maggie's mother. They talked on the phone almost on a daily basis, and since both were active in their local church community, they saw each other at least twice a week at one church event or another. So it wasn't unusual for her mother to be calling, especially now, in the weeks before Christmas, when there were so many holiday events coming up at church. But on this call there weren't the usual pleasantries. Maggie's mother seemed flustered. Finally, she said that earlier in the day, when she was at choir practice, she overheard talk among some of the choir members of Maggie having an ongoing affair with a neighbor. She called her daughter to ask her about the rumors. Maggie felt like everything stopped.

After she hung up the phone, Maggie walked into her kitchen. Her husband and one of her sons, Jack, were just finishing up work on Jack's science project. They both looked up at her quizzically. "What's the matter?" Jack asked. His mother's happy smile could normally charm a grizzly bear, but now her face was stiff and lifeless. Maggie's heart was racing out of control, and her thoughts were not far behind, imagining the consequences of what she had just been told.

Maggie was an extremely popular English teacher at the local elementary school. She had a friendly, bubbly personality, was creative, and enjoyed organizing big parties and social gatherings. She had met her husband when they were both in college, and they fell in love quickly. Their fairy-tale love story led to marriage and a fairy-tale life. Maggie's husband had a successful career in law, and they lived in a charming historic home in their tight-knit community. The couple shared the chores at home on an equal basis and were both fully invested in the lives of their teenage sons. Both children were active hockey players, and the money and time involved in following the two budding stars put a strain on their schedules, but they were committed to their kids and family.

Maggie had always harbored a youthful dream of becoming a famous writer who would tour the world doing book signings. Before they had kids, she had a little writing studio set up in the house, but with a growing family, she had little time to devote to her writing and eventually started to use the space as storage. She met Miles at one of Ben's hockey games. He and his family had moved to town about a year earlier. His wife came to tend to her ailing father, and Miles, being a computer programmer, could work from anywhere, so they settled in and became part of the local community. Jack and Miles's son were in the same class and played together on the hockey team and soon became friends. The boys sometimes traveled to play games in other states. Maggie would often be the one to accompany Jack, while her husband stayed with their other son. She and Miles often found themselves together on these hockey trips, with a lot of time to talk and get to know each other. Miles had shown Maggie some of the computer games he had developed, and she was impressed. She admired that he was able to pursue his dream and earn money following his passion. Miles easily fell for Maggie's vivacious personality. Soon the two had gotten involved romantically. It had been going on for about six months, with them spending time together while the boys played hockey or stealing time during the week to meet for a quick tryst. Both had often talked about leaving their respective partners and starting a new life together. They both felt they were in love. But neither had taken steps in that direction.

Maggie left the kitchen and took a walk around the block. The next day, she called a therapist for an appointment to deal with the train wreck she had set in motion.

STEP ONE: GET A GRIP. Maggie had experience practicing mediation and mindfulness techniques. In fact, about a year earlier, she had even entertained the idea of becoming an instructor. Many of her friends in town actively meditated and practiced mindfulness. Maggie realized her focus had been more on self-realization and pleasure and not on the consequences of these pursuits. Now she faced those consequences. Her affair threatened her family, her relationship with her children, the relationship with many of her friends in town, and the close friendship she had with her mother. She did not know how all these people would react. She assumed that if her mother had found out through the grapevine, then most of her friends in town already knew about the affair as well.

She needed to apply her full attentional resources to deal with this situation.

Maggie started to identify her problem: mixed feelings about her current relationship. She always felt that her feelings were more important to her than social expectations. Thinking through the emotional underpinnings of the situation she now found herself in, she realized that she had had a strict upbringing in a family not used to communicating complaints about each other. Her father was single-minded and did much as he liked, and her mother complied with his wishes. She reflected over how this imbalance in her parent's relationship was always problematic for her and how she felt her mother should have taken better care of herself in the relationship. She had promised herself that she would never lead such a submissive life, and worked hard to avoid this in her own marriage.

Maggie realized that she and her husband had grown apart from each other in putting all their focus on their children's needs and not enough on each other's needs. Neither partner was satisfied with their relationship, but all the focus had been on their children.

STEP TWO: PINPOINT WHAT YOU CAN CONTROL

What couldn't Maggie control? Maggie couldn't control the rumors going around town, nor could she control how people—most importantly, her husband, her kids, and her mother—will react to what she has done. She couldn't control her husband's or Miles' feelings or decisions.

What could Maggie control? Maggie could decide what type of relationship she wanted. Does she want to stay with her husband (if he agrees) and keep her family intact, or does she want to pursue her relationship with Miles? She could explore how she really feels about Miles. Does she love him, or does she love what he represents: the type of life she always wanted but never pursued?

What could she do about the things she couldn't control? While the rumors were out of her control, she could control what she communicates to her mother and what she communicates to her husband and children. She couldn't control her feelings, but she could listen to what her feelings were telling her was right for her. She could seek help from her therapist in clarifying her feelings and working on relationship issues with and without her chosen partner.

STEP THREE: PUSH INTO MOTION. Maggie was really motivated by outside circumstances—she was being forced to address a situation that was no longer secret. She decided to think about her next steps in terms of Easy and Tough Actions. Among the Easy Actions were to reassure her sons that she loved them, to communicate her situation openly and honestly to her mother in person, and to think through how she would communicate her feelings to her husband and Miles.

The Tough Actions would involve resolving in her own mind where her loyalties now lay and her preferred path forward. She was not sure that she could remain in her current relationship even if her husband was understanding of her unfaithfulness. She also felt that she needed to start therapy to look at some of the underlying emotional issues that she had suppressed her entire life—issues that had made it possible for her to act so impulsively in areas that had often gotten her into trouble.

STEP FOUR: PULL BACK. Maggie wanted some time to be alone with her thoughts. She decided to take a few weeks off work and spend some time by herself, reflecting on her values: who she was, what kind of person she wanted to be, who she wanted to be going forward. She realized how much she really missed writing and the freedom she felt when she put her thoughts to paper.

She used to see it as a form of self-therapy. In reflecting on her life, she realized that the life she built—while seemingly happy and stable—didn't leave her room to nurture her creativity and experience a sense of purpose within herself.

She committed to prioritizing the emotional health of her children, since her actions uprooted the family security they had always felt. She decided to cut back some of her community and school obligations and make more time for her sons—and for self-care.

Maggie realized she needed to be kind to herself. Her guilt would often pull at her conscience, but these thoughts were not helpful in improving the situation for anyone involved. She reminded herself that she was a warm, caring person with tremendous empathy and kindness to friend and foe, and these qualities were not automatically eliminated by the events that had led to her midlife crisis.

STEP FIVE: HOLD ON AND LET GO. Maggie held on to the tremendously positive personality traits that made her popular among her friends. At heart, she was an extrovert, agreeable, flexible. She could be funny, silly, serious, and solemn. She would move mountains to help a friend in need and would defend those less fortunate against any form of prejudice. Intellectually, she had tremendous verbal abilities and exhibited creativity both at home with her children and at work with her colleagues. She would hold on to all of these precious talents and let them shine as never before.

At the same time, there were traits that she felt she should downplay. Among them were her tendencies to be impulsive and easily influenced emotionally. She wanted to let go of dishonesty and her tendency to pretend things were okay if they weren't. She would become conscious of how she used feelings of injustice in one context to justify injuries she caused others in a completely different context. She would cultivate being more transparent about her core values and seek to implement them in all of her daily decision-making. She had lost this perspective in her rush through life. She would let go of feelings of having to *hurry up*, and cultivate *taking her time*. This was especially important when interacting with her sons.

Moving forward, Maggie wanted to use this experience to learn about herself and to strive to be the person she wants to be in her new future. She wanted this work to be supervised by a therapist who would more easily see her actions from outside her perspective, which often was so emotionally salient that she could not see the consequences of what her heart was pushing her to do.

Maggie worked to turn her midlife crisis into a positive opportunity by clarifying her life values and goals to see more clearly the future she desired.

Suicide

Kevin and Maureen's Story
Jennifer

Kevin and Maureen had been in love as long as they could remember. They grew up in the same neighborhood, went to the same schools, started dating in high school, and married after college graduation. Maureen had been depressed off and on for years—depression ran in her family—and she experienced seasons of optimism and pleasure and seasons of isolation, crying, irritability, and loss of productivity. Through it all, Kevin was very supportive, even though it took a toll on his well-being over the years. They both wanted kids, but deep down, Maureen was afraid she couldn't be a good mother. Her suicide note was brief.

She wanted Kevin to have a life with someone capable of giving him the family he wanted. In her untreated depression, Maureen didn't realize how happy Kevin was with her, how her presence added to his quality of life in so many ways. In her depression, she couldn't feel his love.

Kevin was so overwhelmed by the news, he simply couldn't tolerate his emotions, and his neighbor gave him a joint. Kevin appreciated how disconnected he felt from reality with cannabis, and it became a regular habit. He just didn't know how else to cope with the pain and couldn't handle the thoughts that went through his mind in the few sober moments of his days.

STEP ONE: GET A GRIP. Kevin was in shock, for sure, but he also realized he was overcome with guilt and self-blame. Thoughts such as *I should have seen this coming; I knew her better than anyone!* and *What should I have done differently?* consumed his waking hours when he wasn't high. So he kept getting high. He was desperately trying to hide from his anger at himself and at Maureen, and he couldn't help but wonder repeatedly, *What happens after death? Is there heaven? Is Maureen okay?* He didn't know whether he should talk to a religious leader or a psychic, but he was afraid of the answers, so back he went for another joint. Kevin both loved and hated the pot; it got him through the moment, but at the same time kept him trapped in the moment, unable to move forward. Kevin realized that getting a grip would require him to stop escaping so he could really pay attention and address all of the questions and feelings that were surfacing. He couldn't commit to giving up the pot, but he did cut down a bit so he could think about his next steps.

STEP TWO: PINPOINT WHAT YOU CAN CONTROL

What couldn't Kevin control? Kevin couldn't control Maureen's actions, her decisions, her depression. He also felt he couldn't control his guilt. He couldn't control whether or not Maureen is in heaven or whether she is "safe."

What could Kevin control? Kevin could control his future, and he supposed he could control his thoughts, but he admitted they were mostly drowned in pot at the moment.

What could he do about the things he couldn't control? Kevin theoretically decided he could find grief support, but he really thought he needed more support in the form of therapy—to learn how to cope with his situation without living in a cloud of pot all day and night and to address his feelings of guilt and anger in a safe place. He could also get support working through the existential questions haunting him about the meaning of life and death.

STEP THREE: PUSH INTO MOTION. Kevin didn't want to push into motion. He preferred the haze of his marijuana. But he also didn't feel like himself. It wasn't like him to escape like this—it felt uncomfortable. He had taken time off work after Maureen's death, but his leave would be ending, and he knew he wouldn't be able to return to work and use pot all day. And he didn't want to stop smoking and return to work and experience the flood of emotions he knew were lurking underneath his high. Finally, with the support of his best friend, he decided to get started. He started with actions that felt easy: setting a daily schedule that involved getting out of bed, showering, eating meals, and doing chores that didn't require thinking. This actually allowed him to start feeling a sense of change—that life might actually be able to go on for him at some point. This shift allowed him to follow his mom's advice and call the local church for a referral for grief support.

Then the cascade of Tough Actions began. He did an online search for therapists, found one who seemed a good fit, called, and made his first appointment.

Kevin was very reluctant to give up cannabis completely. After a few sessions of support, education, and advice, the therapist gave Kevin some homework to think about before the next session. He told Kevin, "Therapy won't work if you're high, so think about whether you want to move forward or be high the rest of your life." This sent Kevin whirling into Step Four.

STEP FOUR: PULL BACK. Kevin started to evaluate who he is now, who he was before Maureen's unexpected death, and what he values. He had an epiphany—that he *can't* understand why she did it and that he didn't see it coming because she didn't want him to. He can't expect himself to understand the inner workings of her mind when she kept her thoughts private. He didn't miss the signs; she protected him. She loved him as much as he loved her. This realization was a game changer for Kevin and helped him stop blaming himself. He realized Maureen knew he loved her and would have done anything to help her. She didn't want the help. He realized that it's okay for him to stop trying to figure out something he can never understand and to accept her decision.

When Kevin told his therapist about his epiphany, he replied, "Good. Now you'll be able to acknowledge and work through the abandonment." Kevin felt his chest tighten, and when he met his therapist's eyes he realized that they both knew that this would take a long time. But Kevin decided he could try to face these feelings and not smother them with pot.

Kevin started thinking about his values, and the two that kept coming to his mind were community and loyalty. He decided to start playing hockey with the guys again and go to the postgame barbecues. He committed to ongoing therapy to work through his feelings about Maureen and to strengthen his ties with his friends and extended family after pushing them away for so long.

STEP FIVE: HOLD ON AND LET GO. Kevin decided he would hold on to the wonderful lifetime of memories he had with Maureen and would learn (through his therapy) to let go of his anger and bitterness that his life didn't turn out the way he thought it would. He decided to hold on to his future by not allowing himself to be lost in drugs, to retreat from life, or to wallow in depression and isolation.

Kevin realized he had to let go of his pride in order to accept the help and support he was being offered by his community without viewing their support as pity; this strengthened his value in community. He also realized holding on to his value of loyalty means actively participating in the lives of his friends and family and letting go of his isolation. He found this helped his focus change a bit; he noticed his focus started shifting away from his pain and on to... life.

Chronic Worry

Howard's Story
Kjell Tore

Howard was an intelligent, accomplished man in his mid-fifties. He was married to Ellen, and the couple had two children who were away at school. Their daughter was getting her doctorate in astronomy and their son was an undergraduate studying botany. Howard had earned a degree in medieval European history and landed a job in Silicon Valley working on search engine technology used to catalog historical artifacts. Ellen was a stay-at-home mom who enjoyed taking care of her family, her house, and her garden. She was an avid horticulturalist and had a range of herbs, vegetables, and flowers growing in their garden and in a large greenhouse.

The couple did not really have any close friends, but enjoyed each other's company. Ellen was a bit more social on her own, and often conferred with other local garden enthusiasts about the best time to plant certain vegetables and about the latest automated watering systems.

Howard and Ellen spent their weekends taking walks through old gold-mining towns close to where they lived in northern California. Howard always had a notebook with him on these excursions, and he would tell people he was working on a book about how these lawless towns functioned without any form of local government.

Howard maintained a very strict daily regimen. He followed a schedule for when he should eat dinner, take his vitamins, spend time reading, and going for walks in the neighborhood. He and Ellen had sex on the first Saturday of every month, which Howard thought was a good arrangement because it simplified something that could get too complicated. These intimate moments coincided with their weekend outings to the abandoned gold-mining towns, so sex usually happened in motel rooms along the interstate highway. Ellen wasn't thrilled with the predictability of their lovemaking and she hated how impersonal the motels felt, but Howard was firm in his routines.

Howard had perfected the art of brooding. He worried about his health, his kids, his car, the chemicals in his toothpaste and the dangers of global warming. He worried about pandemics, nuclear power meltdowns, meteors hitting the earth, and he did not completely discount some of the doomsday scenarios he would read about online. At times, he even felt he could see patterns in news cycles that made him sense something cataclysmic was about to happen. He had a dry sense of humor, and he noticed that when he started talking sarcastically about some of the more outlying topics that concerned him, his colleagues would get nervous and hurry back to their workstations. Despite his quirkiness, he was a valued employee.

Howard's anxiety was overwhelming and he tried to tell himself not to worry about things he had no control over, but when one of his concerns were validated by a news report or a new scientific finding he would spiral down even further into a pit of doom and gloom.

His coping strategy was to fill his days and life with routines and schedules. Predictability seemed to ease his anxiety a bit. When we was in college he did go see a psychiatrist who prescribed antianxiety medication, but Howard didn't like the side effects, so he stopped taking it.

The chronic worrying was causing Howard a great deal of stress and caused many sleepless nights, so at his annual doctor's visit he mentioned it to his physician. The doctor was busy writing on his computer throughout the consultation and barely made any eye contact with Howard. At first Howard was furious. The doctor wasn't taking his concerns seriously; heck, he wasn't even paying attention! But then Howard had a dreadful thought. What if the doctor didn't look at him because there was bad news about his exam? What if there was something seriously wrong with his health that his doctor wasn't telling him? Too distressed to say anything, Howard quickly ended the appointment and left the office.

He returned home in a state of panic and ran to Ellen to tell her his concerns. Ellen tried to reassure him, to no avail. She looked at Howard and shook her head. She couldn't calm him down, so she decided to use this as an opportunity to do something about Howard's worrying and their relationship. She had had enough. She was not happy with how things had been between them since their children moved out. She had heard about the five steps and decided that she and Howard could work through the process for him together.

STEP ONE: GET A GRIP. In a series of discussions with Ellen, Howard came to understand that he had to do something about his worrying and anxieties. This would be his focus moving ahead. He needed to do it for Ellen and his kids, who meant the world to him. And he needed to do it for himself.

Howard realized his problem was a fear of the unknown. This fear was fueled by an underlying anxiety that he had struggled with his entire life. Thinking through the emotional underpinnings of these feelings, he could point out specific episodes in his formative years that gave good reason for being wary and anxious. He remembers how one day while he was walking alone to kindergarten at about age five, an older boy had stopped him on the sidewalk that he took every day to school in a quiet residential area, told him to get down on his knees, and said he was going to slit his throat with a knife he had in his pocket. Howard was traumatized, but never dared to tell anyone about the experience. The memory was etched into his psyche: not only *could* the unthinkable happen, but it *had* happened. And it could happen again. He also mused about stories he had heard of several family members on his father's side who struggled with anxiety and depression, so he thought that this could be an inherited vulnerability. In fact, one of his uncles had taken his own life in his thirties, but nobody in the family knew the exact circumstances.

STEP TWO: PINPOINT WHAT YOU CAN CONTROL

What couldn't Howard control? Howard understood that he couldn't control the unknown or future catastrophic events impacting him or his family members. He did not have control over his wife's feelings for him, and he did not think he would be able to control his constant anxious ruminations and flights of suspicion.

What could Howard control? Howard had control over many aspects of his life. He had good daily routines, some of which had been put in place in an attempt to control uncertainties and unknowns. His routines and rituals had given him some degree of foreseeability, but they did not seem to be sufficient to quiet his worrying mind. He enjoyed plenty of physical and intellectual activities and challenges that made his life meaningful. And he had control over his contribution in his life in partnership with his wife, whom he loved dearly.

What could he do about the things he couldn't control? Howard knew that he had to find a way to deal with his fear of the unknown and the uncertainties driving his worrying. Getting help with these difficulties might also result in better sleep quality, as well. He realized that his daughter was very much like him, and he wanted to talk to her about his problems with anxiety. Ellen had heard from their son that their daughter seemed to have a drinking problem, and he was worried that she might be using alcohol to regulate a similar disposition for worrying.

STEP THREE: PUSH INTO MOTION. In general, Howard was very personable and always open to discussing interesting topics. He understood his wife's concerns when she communicated them clearly to him. His love for her gave him the motivation he needed to do something about his fragile mental state.

Howard divided what he needed to do going forward into Easy and Tough Actions. Among the Easy Actions were contacting a new doctor who could refer him to a good psychiatrist who could provide guidance on natural medicines that could help reduce his high anxiety level. He was hesitant to take pharmaceuticals again because of the side effects he experienced years ago, so he wanted to try herbal and homeopathic options. He decided to ask Ellen to accompany him to his appointments. She knew a lot about herbs and maybe she could help him do some research. He would ask her if he could help her in the garden and maybe they could cultivate some herbs that would help relive his anxiety. He also decided that he would work on developing a network of friends so as not to be so dependent on Ellen.

Among the Tough Actions was learning to communicate better with his wife about his fears and anxieties and about emotional issues in general. But he didn't know where to start. He thought they could work with a therapist to learn how to communicate with each other more openly. With a therapist they could also bring up sexual issues that he always felt were awkward to talk about. He now understood how important this was for Ellen and he felt ashamed that he had insisted on his routine for so many years. He was excited to work with someone who could help them make their relationship stronger. Ellen was the love of his life and he wanted to make sure she was happy.

STEP FOUR: PULL BACK. It was time for Howard to pull back and reflect on the many blessings in his life: his wife, his children, and his sharp intellect that had given him such an interesting career. Looking at the big picture, he felt he had so much to live for and be happy about, and this reinforced his commitment to making the choices and taking actions to help him deal with his anxiety issues. His efforts to alleviate his condition might also benefit his daughter; he could share his experience and perhaps help her avoid the emotional struggle that he suffered with for too long.

He was determined that these efforts to change his thinking patterns were not put on the shoulders of his loving wife. It was up to him to take the steps needed to gain more balance in his life. He needed to learn to master his anxieties on his own and not depend on Ellen to adapt to his needs. A better balance in his own mental state would allow him to reach out to Ellen on a more mutually agreeable basis.

STEP FIVE: HOLD ON AND LET GO. Thinking through the positive personality traits that he wanted to hold on to and cultivate,

Howard recognized he had always been a very meticulous and conscientious individual. There had always been an order and self-discipline about his behavior. Being a dependable partner and colleague, he carried out the obligations he agreed to faithfully and responsibly, with the modesty of a dedicated friend. These were the endearing qualities that Ellen saw in her husband. He would hold on to these important traits.

As with any positive quality, too much can be a negative. He decided to try to let go of being too rigid, inflexible, and perfectionistic. He knew it would take a while for him to do much about these tendencies without professional help, but recognizing them was a good start. He was learning how excessive outward control is often interpreted as cold and heartless, which didn't characterize Howard at all. He decided to make a conscious effort to be more flexible and spontaneous in the future.

Moving forward, Howard realized he will benefit from staying focused in the present in his personal interactions with his family, and not letting his mind wander into future uncertainties—not only for the sake of Ellen and the kids, but for the sake of his own quality of life.

Spiritual Crisis

Dave's Story
Jennifer

Dave was forty years old and about to be married. He was also depressed and filled with angst. He appeared pale, exhausted, stressed. His stomach was always giving him trouble, and he was losing weight. He loved his fiancée, but as the wedding date approached, his condition only worsened. That nagging feeling—the

one he had ignored since age eleven—was rising to his surface, re-
fusing to be pushed aside.

Dave grew up in a happy bubble. His family attended a large
church with a sizable youth group, and his childhood and teen
years were spent with his church friends—at Bible studies,
summer camps, and volunteer service trips. He always loved
singing, and there were fifty kids in the church youth choir. They
did everything together. They went on spiritual prayer retreats,
made crafts with the elders, mentored younger children, and
played sports together. His entire life revolved around his youth
group and church. He read his Bible, memorized Bible verses,
and learned all of the stories in the Old and New Testaments. He
loved his community bubble; it kept him from getting into trouble at school and at home. He wasn't partying, got pretty decent
grades, and was known for being respectful to adults and nice
to all the other kids at school. He was happy.

After college, when all of his friends started getting married,
he took an international business job, dividing his time between Santa Barbara and Hong Kong. When his friends started
having kids and asking when he was going to settle down, his
career took off, and he spent more and more time overseas, focusing on learning Cantonese fluently. For years his family
dropped hints—his mom wanted grandkids, after all—and every
time he returned home, his parents seemed to have a dinner
party filled with eligible women from church. One stood out
clearly from the rest: a gorgeous blonde with eyes the color of
the ocean, a kind heart, and an infectious laugh. Dave was
drawn to her immediately.

They had been dating for eighteen months (in between multiple business trips) when Dave decided to propose. Their
families threw an enormous engagement party, and the wedding
planning began. Dave still had the familiar nagging feeling, but
he was caught up in a wonderful companionship and the happi-

ness he saw in his family every time he was home. But when he would leave for Hong Kong, the internal nagging feeling resurfaced, and he would spend enormous amounts of time trying to shove it away. It grew and grew.

For nearly thirty years, Dave had known he was gay. He knew it as instinctively as he knew air was for breathing. He also knew that everything he had been taught told him it was a sin to be gay. Marriage was ordained by God, meant to be entered into by a man and a woman. He also knew it was meant to be forever: divorce was also not part of God's plan, and as his wedding was coming together, Dave was falling apart.

STEP ONE: GET A GRIP. Dave had known for quite some time deep down inside that his main problem was the contrast between his belief system and his biology. He shared the faith of his entire extended family. Every life lesson he knew was birthed in scripture. Everything he thought about the world—structure, order, morality, spirituality—seemed in jeopardy because of who he knew he really was. He identified two key issues: (1) "On my own spiritual journey, can I be saved and gay?" He feared losing his relationship with God. (2) "Will I be exiled from my family, my extended family, my church family, the choir, the service groups, the prayer group?" He feared losing the only life he had ever known.

STEP TWO: PINPOINT WHAT YOU CAN CONTROL

What couldn't Dave control? He knew he couldn't control being gay or how others would react when he came out.

What could Dave control? It was up to Dave to decide whether to go through with his wedding and marriage. He could give himself space and remove the pressure of the pending calendar date, stepping off the conveyor belt carrying him toward his wedding. He could address his symptoms of anxiety and depression. He could learn about better self-care since he was so worried every-one would leave him.

What could he do about the things he couldn't control? Dave de-cided that he could seek therapy as well as spiritual guidance from someone safe and nonjudgmental. He could decide when, if, and how to come out, and to whom, when he felt ready.

STEP THREE: PUSH INTO MOTION. Dave was falling apart and knew he couldn't go on like this. His desire to *somehow* end decades of internalized angst motivated him to take the steps that seemed easiest. He wasn't ready to talk to his family or friends about any of this, so he decided to consult with a psychiatrist regard-ing treatment options for depression and anxiety and to discuss how therapy might be of benefit. He learned about relaxation training for anxiety, different types of therapy, and medication options for treating his symptoms, and he was given a few names of therapists in the area who specialized in life tran-sitions. He started doing some breathing techniques the doctor taught him, which gave him a glimmer of hope that he could get through this. He also started to research gay-friendly churches, and he began studying the theology of a few different denomi-nations as a first step in exploring how his faith and sexuality might coexist.

As his first tough action, Dave ended his engagement. He wasn't yet ready to disclose his reason, but he was able to hon-estly say the relationship didn't feel right for him. His family was disappointed but respectful, and he felt relieved by creating for himself ample time and the emotional space to figure out his the-ology and to prepare for the reaction of the conservative community he loved so well when he was ready to come out. At this point, he wasn't ready to address the other Tough Actions he anticipated. He wanted to spend time in thought, in therapy, an in prayer.

STEP FOUR: PULL BACK. Dave spent time identifying his personal core values: integrity and honesty, showing kindness and love with acts of service, and worshiping God. He thought about whether he would lose these values—which he felt were rooted in his church upbringing—by being openly gay. With reflection he realized that he was actually being *more* honest with himself now than he ever had been and that for him working the Five Steps and calling off his wedding were acts of integrity. He felt he would still be able to continue to serve others and worship God, but he thought he'd have to devote some time to a search for a similar church community that would accept him.

While he was starting therapy, he decided to simplify his schedule by cutting out singing in the church choir because it started to make him feel self-conscious. He said, "I don't want to literally be on stage while I'm processing this!" He continued to volunteer doing yard work for homebound elders in his church community when he was home from Hong Kong.

Dave also started evaluating some of his relationships. Two of his friends were overly harsh with him when he canceled the wedding. He thought about what each had said. He thought one was clearly projecting his own issues onto Dave (what he said to Dave wasn't about Dave at all, but about himself), and the other was simply unkind in how he voiced his criticism. Dave decided to pull back from these friendships.

Finally, Dave asked himself whether his internal dialog (his thought life) matched his core values. He decided to make these values his focus and cut out negative thought patterns that didn't reflect them. He decided he needed to treat himself like he treated others: with kindness.

STEP FIVE: HOLD ON AND LET GO. Dave decided to hold on to his core values and let go of trying to be something he knows he is not. He decided to hold on to his faith and to keep trusting in God, even if the people in his church treated him with judgment and exile. He decided to focus his faith on God, not on other humans. In doing so, he let go of his long-standing belief that he was inherently flawed and held on to his belief that he was a child of God, made in God's own image. He let go of dwelling on how he wished things could have been in his life and held on to what he felt was the big picture: "I worship a loving God."

Conclusion:
From Pain to Sane

Jennifer

I HAVE A FRIEND WHO'S an anesthesiologist, which basically means he renders people unconscious for a living, which is the exact opposite of what I do (I hope). I told him I was writing this chapter with one question in mind: *How do you convince someone who has been chronically suffering to make seemingly uncomfortable lifestyle changes—changes that may take weeks to months to manifest any results?* Here is his response (and yes, this is a direct quote from my Facebook Messenger). I've named this rant "The Pumpkin Spice Latte at the End of the Rainbow."

> It's hard to wait for sleep hygiene results, but sometimes there is an unbearably long line at Starbucks for your 900-calorie pumpkin spice frappe. Do you still soldier on, knowing you will be flanked by people who are sucking up your 5G bandwidth and wearing disagreeable perfume, and shouting into the phone? Yes.

Yes you will. Because it's Autumn, and you're a basic
human. You have already proven that you have the
mental wherewithal to endure this kind of adversity to
get an overpriced seasonal beverage that is never as sat-
isfying as you think it will be, so why wouldn't you
show that same kind of patience and mental toughness
in sticking to a plan that is going to benefit you in so
many ways? I mean its sleep! You don't even have to
stand up and shuffle forward like a zombie like you do
in a metropolitan coffeehouse. You just have to be su-
pine and follow your psychiatrist's instructions and
shut your fucking phone off. Maybe have a little sex
first. How hard could that be? You're absolutely ready
to take this journey!—Casey Husser, MD

Casey and I go way back—to childhood—and he's a go-getter.
He has a mindset I've always admired. But his sense of sarcasm
(which I adore) doesn't necessarily resonate with the people in
crisis I see on a daily basis. I suppose there's a reason he's an
anesthesiologist and I'm a psychiatrist. So while I do appreciate
his sarcastic input, let's think about this a little differently.

There are two types of swimmers in the world: those who
jump straight into the pool and the temperature checkers who
dip some fingers or toes into the pool while internally weighing the pros and cons of going in. Some of us are wired to
welcome swift and bold change, and others of us prefer to step
into things, to commit in small pieces before reaching the final
goal, going slow enough to turn back before it's too late. Who-
mever you are, whichever style suits you, you can adopt the
recommendations in this chapter and feel better again. There's
hope for us all... even those of us who despise changing habits,
who feel every desired change is an internal battle between
what we *want* to do and what we *really want* to do. (For exam-

ple, I *want* to cut calories and eat more vegetables, but what I *really want* is to open my refrigerator and see cheese and wine.) It just takes a little motivation, and if you have a really stubborn brain, you can even use the Five Steps to make these changes.

There have been countless books written on adrenal stress and fatigue; this isn't meant to be one of them. However, we do want you to have some easy-to-follow steps to counteract the physical symptoms of chronic stress. After reading "The Science of Stress" chapter, you know why you have them; now let's get rid of them. Keep in mind that if your symptoms are so severe that these recommendations don't help all of them or if you are too overwhelmed by what you read, you can seek personal medical help from a functional or integrative medicine specialist or naturopath doctor.

We're going to target five key symptoms: muscle tension, salt cravings, sugar cravings and weight gain, immune system and libido problems, and insomnia and fatigue. You can refer to "The Science of Stress" chapter if you want to remember why you have the symptoms; that may also give you some motivation for making the desired changes.

Muscle Tension

When the human body spends too much time in the fight-or-flight mode, with multiple adrenaline rushes that aren't followed by running from a bear, the result is muscle tension, jitteriness, and frustration (physical and emotional). This muscle tension can even reignite old injuries—in the back and neck, especially—causing further frustration and pain.

Here's the science behind it (it'll only take fifteen seconds, I swear): Remember from "The Science of Stress" chapter, parts of the movement center of the brain—the two basal ganglia—are also involved in stress management. When the basal ganglia are overactive, people tend to feel like their engines are revving up all the time: they anticipate the worst outcome and they might feel anxious, worried, or even panicky. The two basal ganglia (one on the right side of the brain and one on the left), which serve as the connection between the musculoskeletal system and stressful emotions, can be the gateway to treating chronic physical tension as well as anxiety. Learning to decrease the stress in your life will help lessen physical pain and working on the muscle tension will help lower stress. *(End of science.)*

If you've ever felt amazing after a fabulous massage, you'll understand. When you pull the tension out of your body, it comes out of your brain, too. It all comes back in time, of course, and most of us can't afford daily massages, but there are other things we can do.

Let's talk about *movement*. (I am intentionally not using the word *exercise*, because very few of you would cheer and the majority would throw this book across the room and tell me to "F-off" if I did.) So we may not feel up to exercising, but we all like to *move*, don't we? It just feels good to get up and walk across the room when you've been sitting too long. Now the jump-in-the-pool people may want to run off to the gym and lift weights for hours a day, but if you're suffering with a lot of chronic tension or pain, this is the time to be gentle on your body, but do get moving. Remember, adrenaline and cortisol are there to make us move (run from the bear), so being sedentary will allow them to keep circulating and the tension will keep building. Movement will actually allow them to be flushed out of the body. (Doesn't that sound nice?)

Here are some suggestions for easing both the brain and the body:

- Take a five- or ten-minute power walk a few times throughout the day. It will help relieve tension, change your breathing pattern, and give your mind a few minutes away from the task at hand.
- Consider trying acupuncture.
- Try a few gentle yoga classes. For those who don't have access, you can find restorative yoga classes online. With a yoga mat, a few blankets, and a bolster (that's a yoga pillow), you'll be ready to roll. It's often helpful to do a few relaxing poses right before going to bed to help with sleep. Just don't do any positions that hurt.
- Get regular light massages if you can afford them.
- Take baths with lavender Epsom salts. Lavender is a scent known to induce relaxation, and Epsom salts contain magnesium, which is an excellent muscle relaxer.
- Try some guided meditations. There are countless apps and online sources you can use for free. Many of my patients like listening to Michael Sealey, who has dozens of free guided meditations on YouTube that address insomnia, overthinking, letting go of past relationships, positive healing energy, and other topics.

In addition to the suggestions from the list above, you can also try some breathing techniques. I use two. The first is belly breathing. When we're stressed, we tend to breathe from our chests (which is what we do when we run). However, relaxing breaths come from the belly. Lay down with one hand on your chest and the other on your belly. As you breathe, the hand on your chest should remain still and the hand on your belly should rise and fall with your breaths. This takes practice despite how simple it sounds. Relax your entire abdomen and pelvic floor (stop clenching that pelvic floor!) and picture a string pulling your belly button out as you inhale. Belly breathing can be done anywhere—in your car, in a meeting, on the phone, when you wake during the night. The technique, when done properly, can even help with panic attacks. It's worth practicing it several times throughout the day.

The second breathing technique I use is sometimes used in yoga practice. It's based on the medical principles that induce panic in many first-year medical students who—as soon as they acquire their first stethoscope—listen to the human heart for the first time, discover it to be irregular, and self-diagnose themselves with an arrhythmia. The reality is that the human heart rate changes with inhalation and exhalation. When we inhale the heart beats faster, and when we exhale it slows. This is controlled by the vagus nerve, and in yoga, the vagus nerve is seen as the mediator between the states of fight-or-flight and rest-and-digest. The technique is meant to bring the body's physiology into a restful place. There are several different methods for this; the one I use is simple. Inhale while slowly counting to four, exhale while slowly counting to six. Do not hold your breath in after you inhale; immediately begin to exhale. Once you have the hang of it (your exhalation is longer than your inhalation), then after you exhale completely, count to two before inhaling again. Four counts in, six counts out, two counts of pause, then repeat. It takes a little practice, and different people have different speeds of counting, which is fine. Use the speed that relaxes you most.

This all goes back to the feedback loop between the brain and muscles. Calming the body calms the brain, and calming the brain calms the body.

Salt Cravings

Remember from "The Science of Stress" chapter, in an acute crisis, our bodies retain salt, which helps us hold on to water, which keeps our blood pressure up so we can run from danger. Often, in times of chronic stress, the opposite can happen: our bodies can't hold on to salt, which means we lose water (through urination), resulting in dehydration and dizziness upon standing.

Often when people start getting dizzy and feel dehydrated, they turn to electrolyte sports drinks thinking they are aiding rehydration. However, sports drinks were developed for athletes who need a push during an *acute* body crisis (rushing ten yards to thrust one's head into someone else's head, for example, which I do not recommend), not a *chronic* body crisis (like fighting mononucleosis for six months), so they tend to be high in sugar and have an electrolyte balance designed to help the adrenal gland's response to *acute* stress. This just worsens the electrolyte imbalance brought on by chronic stress, leading to more salt cravings, more water loss, and more dizziness.

You may need to be a little more generous with the saltshaker if you're craving salt and having dizzy spells (particularly upon standing). If this symptom persists over time, consult your doctor for blood pressure checks. Avoid salty, empty-of-nutrition snacks. Keep your diet healthy and add a little salt to your meals, making sure your water intake is sufficient. Skip the chips.

Sugar Cravings and Weight Gain

Cortisol is the culprit here. When you're walking home from the neighborhood Halloween party and get approached by some intoxicated guy wearing a Hello Kitty mask, cortisol will make sure your muscles have the maximum amount of energy they can get in case you need to fight him off. This energy is in the form of glucose, or sugar. It is fast burning and will be your best bet in sidestepping that intoxicated Hello Kitty loser. When our crisis state is chronic, cortisol can't keep up, but our bodies still think we need sugar for fast energy, so we crave it and eat it, leading to sugar rushes and crashes, followed by more cravings, rushes, and crashes. All this excess sugar gets pumped into our tissues and stored as fat, leading to that muffin top, jowls, or panda belly.

As mentioned in "The Science of Stress" chapter, cortisol will be elevated early in times of adrenal stress and tends to lower over time. When it is elevated, exercise (sorry—I mean *movement*) will help flush it out. Take the sugar out of your life and eat a diet balanced with healthy proteins and *lots* of vegetables, a little bit of complex carbohydrates, and healthy fats.

The supplement L-theanine (from green tea) can help to blunt the effect of cortisol (and 200 mg of L-theanine twice daily can also contribute to better sleep). Ashwagandha (from the roots and berries of an evergreen shrub that grows in India) can also help regulate cortisol when that "wired-and-tired" stage sets in—when you need energy but are also revved up by stress. My colleague, author Dr. Kabran Chapek, swears that laughing lowers cortisol levels during stress. What's the harm in giving it a try?

Immune System and Libido Problems

These take time to fix, because cortisol needs to be balanced for the immune system to return to normal and the adrenal glands won't produce the hormones you need until the brain turns off the distress signal. Rest when you're sick, use the techniques outlined in the book to lower stress (mindfulness, breathing techniques, guided meditations, yoga, and even therapy), and as your adrenal stress is treated, your immune and libido problems should subside. You can support your immune system with vitamin C (up to two or three grams daily), vitamin D (check your level—the cutoff for "sufficient" is 30ng/dL, but boosting to 60-

8ong/dL can help with immunity and mood), and the mineral zinc (30 to 60mg daily, in divided doses to avoid stomach upset). You can also talk to your functional or integrative medicine specialist, your general practitioner or naturopathic doctor about checking hormone levels and when to seek treatment (for hormone replacement therapy, for example) if your crisis is really long-lasting. Be patient. It won't be forever.

Insomnia and Fatigue

Fatigue is rooted in many things: muscle tension, poor diet, changes in physiology (see "The Science of Stress" chapter), sugar crashes, and disrupted sleep. As we learned in that first chapter, sometimes when we experience chronic stress cortisol can spike too late at night (causing a "second wind" of energy that makes going to bed difficult) and sometimes it dips at the wrong time, causing the victim to wake during the night in a panic, sweating and tense, due to a resulting sudden drop in the blood sugar level. If you're waking up in a panic, you may want to try having a small snack before bed, such as a few walnuts, a spoonful of nut butter, or a small piece of cheese. This gives you fat and protein to help maintain an even blood sugar level throughout the night. Do *not* have sugary snacks such as ice cream or cookies. Those will make you feel worse.

The best way to regulate sleep is discipline, which is everyone's favorite word, right? Remember, as humans we are highly trainable and can learn to sleep through the night as adults, just as we did as infants. This is referred to in medicine as "sleep hygiene," which to me sounds incredibly boring and doesn't nearly reflect the effort it takes. So I call it "sleep boot camp," which I think accurately reflects how fun it is, but the end result is a quality of sleep that prepares you for daily life. It's totally worth it.

Dr. Love's Sleep Boot Camp

ESTABLISH A SLEEP SCHEDULE AND STICK WITH IT—SEVEN DAYS A WEEK. This is the hardest part initially. If you need to arise at 6 A.M., you need to be *asleep* by 10 P.M. at the latest. Pick a reasonable eight- or nine-hour window that works during the week, and stick with it on the weekends, too. I know it hurts to think about waking up early on weekends, but if you really want to improve the quality of your sleep and improve your overall energy level, it's a necessary component. The more you do it, the easier it gets. (Note: If you are in massive adrenal fatigue and need to be under the care of a physician, you will likely need to get all the sleep you can initially. But once your adrenal glands start healing, start using the sleep schedule to train your brain into healthy habits.)

NO CAFFEINE TEN HOURS BEFORE YOUR BEDTIME. That's right—ten hours. You may be able to get away with eight hours, but start with ten and don't waver until you're sleeping like a baby angel all night. I hear all the time: "But I can drink a cup of coffee and fall asleep right away!" Or "Caffeine doesn't affect me." Caffeine is proven to cause wakefulness, and if you are so tired you fall asleep after drinking it, the quality of your sleep is being affected. Our brains need to experience certain stages of sleep during the night in order to rest and renew our bodies for the day ahead. Caffeine disrupts the normal sleep stage transitions, and we spend less time in the much-needed deep stages of sleep with caffeine in our systems. If you don't feel rested, caffeine is a likely culprit.

NO NAPS. Sleep *only* during your set sleep hours. If you nap, your brain will struggle to slide into deep sleep that night. If you're tired at 4 P.M., push through it; eventually, your brain will learn when to sleep and how to follow the necessary sleep stages during those set sleep hours. (Again, if you're under the care of a physician for severe fatigue, this rule may be postponed until you are more stable.)

NO ELECTRONICS ONE HOUR BEFORE BED. Don't whine (yes, I can hear you groaning)—I'm being generous here. Ideally, you should probably put your phone away and log off your computer three hours before going to bed. (One hour sounds more reasonable now, right?) Some studies have shown that people who read e-books at bedtime get about forty-five minutes less sleep per night than those who read traditional books. The short wavelength of artificial blue light stimulates your brain, and your phone is so addicting that you can scroll for an hour and not realize it. Put it away.

DO NOT USE ALCOHOL TO FALL ASLEEP. You're not alone if you do: this is a common mistake people make. Alcohol is known to disrupt the normal patterns of sleep. It is a sedative, and yes, it will sedate you, but as your liver metabolizes alcohol and your blood alcohol level decreases over time, your nervous system starts to experience the opposite symptom—stimulation. This can mean anything from disrupted sleep to tossing and turning, to less time spent in deep sleep, to actual waking and—in more severe cases—tremors, muscle twitching, and agitation. Repeat after me: Alcohol is the frenemy of sleep.

Follow these steps and in a matter of weeks, you'll start to feel more refreshed than you have in a long time.

Some Final Words on Fatigue and Relaxation

Each of the symptoms we've touched on can occur independently or in clusters. The symptoms I see most commonly are anxiety, exhaustion, and difficulty relaxing. So in addition to everything you've already read in this book, there are a few easy tips to keep in mind to aid in relaxation even when relaxation feels emotionally impossible. It all starts with using the five senses. If the brain is wired to pick up on distress and activate a cascade of physiologic changes in response, then it must be wired to pick up on relaxing cues that can help turn off the system, right? The hypothalamus senses the environment, so think about creating an environment that engulfs the five senses.

Sight. Light a candle, watch a fire in the fireplace, take time to enjoy a sculpture or painting, or even create an inspiration board with photos or magazine pictures that evoke a sense of calm and hang it where you'll see it regularly.

Smell. Vanilla and lavender are known for their ability to calm; you can find relaxing scents in candles, essential oils, lotions, herbal teas, or your morning cup of coffee. (I don't recommend drinking much caffeine during a crisis, but a few ounces of coffee in the morning can start the day if it doesn't make you anxious, and the smell is divine.) You can use eucalyptus and lavender in essential oil shower sprays. (A few sprays into the warm shower before you get in creates a wonderful, relaxing shower.) You can also find nice essential oils for taking baths (which also hits the sense of touch).

Sound. I love the sound of running water—the ocean, a stream, even a fountain. There are apps that recreate just about any sound you might find relaxing, from wind to rain to forest sounds. You also can put on your favorite songs, have a white noise machine in the background, and listen to guided meditations. (Sometimes I just enjoy the sound of silence.)

TASTE. This can be really fun: take the time to savor your food, bite by bite. Indulge in a small piece of dark chocolate, and savor it on your tongue. Consciously remember to enjoy your food.

TOUCH. Think fuzzy socks, a weighted blanket, a soft flannel shirt, having someone massage your feet. I have several dresses that are totally professional, but they're so soft I feel like I'm wearing pajamas all day. Pick your fabrics. Maybe invest in some soft (or flannel) sheets. Maybe you enjoy walking through your garden and feeling your flowers and leaves or the warmth of a mug of hot tea on a cold day.

AS YOU ARE WORKING through your Five Steps, healing and growing through your life crisis, remember to use these tools to help restore physical and emotional well-being. You can do this.

Postscript:
The COVID-19 Diaries

DESPITE LIVING ON SEPARATE CONTINENTS (Jennifer in North America and Kjell Tore in Northern Europe), we both struggled through the trials and tribulations of the pandemic and had to deal with the international upheaval left in its wake. Here is a short overview of our experiences applying the Five Steps in our own lives during the pandemic crisis of 2020.

My COVID Crisis
Kjell Tore

The drastic measures of closing schools, stopping travel, and minimizing contact with the elderly were imposed in Norway in early March 2020. It was still the middle of winter here in Norway with ice on the lakes, snow in the mountains, and the town full of ski tourists. At the time, I was working at two separate psychiatric wards in a hospital about an hour away from my home in Lillehammer. One of the wards treats young people with early symptoms of psychosis (thought disorder) and the other treats older people with early signs of dementia. Even though direct patient contact was reduced to urgent care, I continued to drive to work on a daily basis throughout the period to help as needed. The morning drive along Lake Mjøsa was toward the sun rising in the east and the drive home in the evening was toward the sun setting in the west down between the mountains, often with spectacular displays of light across the lake in both directions. The entire stretch of road was being upgraded from one to two lanes, however, so frequent detours and stops gave me a chance to get plenty of practice doing the breathing techniques I use for strressful situations at the hospital.

My mother, who is seventy-nine years old, was stuck in her home in California when the shelter-in-place order was issued. She could not travel to Norway and I could not travel to the United States. I was worried about her, but my daughter was studying at a university close to her house in California, so I knew she was not alone if she needed help.

Here in Lillehammer, we were allowed to go for walks and ski on the mountains but it had to be alone. We were not permitted to see friends, go to the gym, or visit restaurants.

From Day 1 of the COVID crisis, I applied the Five Steps to my life and my daily schedule. It worked out well, because Jennifer and I were reading through the edits for this book at the same time. It gave me a chance to really think about the steps and how to use them practically in a life-changing crisis lasting over a period of months.

STEP 1: GET A GRIP. Having traveled on transatlantic flights since I was two years old, my first impulse when our prime minister announced the emergency on TV was to look up, expecting oxygen masks to drop down from an overhead compartment. Nothing popped out. I wouldn't say it was a letdown, but I think the kid in me was hoping that I would finally get to try on those yellow masks and orange vests (with bright red whistles dangling) that were reserved for the crew on normal flights and passengers only in emergencies. I remember the stewardesses always saying, "In case of emergency, stay calm and make sure you put the yellow mask on yourself first so you can breathe properly, then help others who might need help." Right, so in reality I had trained for this crisis since I was about two years old.

To externalize the drama of the moment and to help me gain a grip of the situation, I identified the main problem I was facing: lack of control. Control has always been an issue in my life. My father let me down in my childhood when my parents divorced and he started one company after another without time for me, so I developed a hard shell that refused to trust anyone other than myself. The emotional response became a need to control situations in a way that would protect me from broken expectations. My good fortune was that I had many loving and dependable adults in my life (mom, uncles, and aunts), who always exceeded my expectations, so I have nothing to complain about. Yet, there was something very powerful about those early negative experiences with my father that I have never quite been able to shake.

The flipside of control is trust. To me, if you hand over control to someone else, that is a sign that you trust that person. My time here in Norway had given me such a good experience with the system of government that I confidently put my trust in the authorities to make the right decisions for the country and my family during this crisis. This confidence in the system made it easier for me to relax about handing over any freedom of movement, and let me focus on getting on with the business of making the most out of a difficult situation.

STEP 2: PINPOINT WHAT YOU CAN CONTROL
What couldn't I control? I had no control over the restrictions on travel imposed by the government, nor on all the other re-

strictions imposed by the authorities. There was no indication how long the restrictions would last, but we expected them to last a few months. And we could not control the when and where of being struck by an unseen microbe, especially since I was at work at the hospital almost daily, and several colleagues and patients at the hospital had tested positive. I fully accepted the risk of possibly contracting the virus, but would take all the precautions that were prescribed for us to follow. One worry was how the crisis would affect our patient group, many of whom were becoming increasingly anxious and depressed because of their isolated situation.

What could I control? I could control a lot of things (I'm good and relatively disciplined at it), so it was a joy to think of new routines and habits in the days to come. I could stop watching the news on television and just get the news on my phone so I could keep updated on international events and the spread of the virus in California where my mother was living. I could find new ways of socializing and communicating with friends on the Internet, and learn to use these platforms. And I could be present for my youngest son and check in with my oldest kids, who were away studying at university.

What could I do about the things I couldn't control? The most serious worry was my mother living alone in her house in California. She belonged to a group described as "vulnerable," and spikes of the virus had been reported in Los Angeles, not far from where she lived. I could call her a few times a day to check on her, and I could communicate with my daughter, who could visit her. I encouraged my mother to stay safe and self-isolate, but I knew she would be making her own decisions regardless of what I said. In terms of my family here in Norway, I was confident that the government had good control of the situation, and I kept updated on the rules we needed to follow. Most of our patients could be followed up via telemedicine, which turned out to be an effective way to monitor them to see that they were doing well.

Financially, the loss of rental income because of the travel restrictions was a blow to me. The short-term rental income had been a way to keep the family house where all three of my children spent their early years. I could not sustain the mortgage without rental income over time. I had to consider selling the house, and worried about how the kids would feel about it.

STEP 3: PUSH INTO MOTION. One of the first decisions I made was to be as positive as I could during this period. There was so much for me to be thankful for—my family, friends and I were healthy, safe, and living in one of the most caring and well-organized countries in the world. I had no right to exude doom and gloom, and felt it was my obligation to do my part to generate as many smiles and positive vibes as possible. I didn't have much social contact, but I was regularly on the computer and phone to talk with my mother and friends in Norway and abroad. When I came to my office in the morning, there was a lady in the next building with a window facing the entryway. I started to wave and smile at her every morning when I arrived at work. She probably thought I was totally wacky, but she started waving after the first week and then both waving and smiling after two weeks. Persistence is golden.

My Easy Actions: It was easy for me to call my mother often and find out how she was doing. We got much closer during these frequent conversations. She was coping wonderfully. Two neighbors came over to her house regularly to practice tai chi—appropriately socially distanced—in her garden, and my daughter visited her frequently to bring her food and any medicines as needed. Close friends of the family called to check on her as well.

Here in Lillehammer, I ordered a food service that delivers ingredients and accompanying recipes (literally with step-by-step instructions), so I could cook my own meals. I am not a good cook, but this gave me the opportunity to learn to make some fancy dishes with unusual vegetables and sauces. My youngest son didn't appreciate the vegetables and sauces though, so I would leave those out for him. I also installed some pull-up bars in the doorway to my bedroom and started a daily exercise session including pull-ups, push-ups, and aerobic training in an annex to my house. A yoga mat was always rolled out on my living room floor, so I could lie down and stretch my back and do some meditation or yoga when I got home from work. About once a week, I ran up to the Olympic ski jump (1994 Lillehammer Games), which is close by, and walked the 1,000 stairs it takes to get to the top. That was my weekly Rocky rush.

In addition to my daily work schedule at the hospital, I thought I needed something a bit different and silly to think about to stimulate my mind in the evenings. After Jennifer started an Instagram account, I thought I should start one too to help promote this book. I wanted to be able to visualize the various principles Jennifer and I write about with some simple photo or visual meme. There were some Easter decorations lying around in my dining room (Easter was just four weeks into the shelter-in-place order). The common Easter tradition for Norwegians is skiing in the mountains, but this year—despite the gorgeous weather—we were encouraged to stay at home. So I was at home with Easter decoration, one of which was an entire box of little pink chicks. I first bunched them together into a group on the dining room table, then hung a straggler over on a pineapple in a fruit bowl on the table—I thought of that pink chick as the rebel! It may seem odd for a grown man to be playing with pink chicks, but they were cute. And silly. And just the intellectual challenge I needed.

The next day I hung a few of the chicks on a decorative tree with lighted branches sticking out in all directions in the corner of my dining room—it struck me that they seemed to be practicing social distancing. I took a picture of it and sent it to my mom. The next day I published it on Instagram and that was the start of the Pink Chicks saga. Every day since, I have been publishing one or two on the sites @hovikphd and @the.pinkchicks, and will continue to do so until the book is published.

During this time I was also planning a clinical study of the five-step model together with a good friend of mine who is professor of psychology at the university here in town. He took his PhD at the same time as I did and on the same project, so we know each other really well. We were both excited about doing research on the model, and are developing specialized test instruments for the outcome measures with various professors around the world to be able to measure the effect of using the steps compared to other interventions. Updates on this research activity will be published on the website www.lovehovik.com

My Tough Actions: It was difficult to think about selling my children's childhood house. I would have to talk to them about it before I made any final decision.

I was feeling quite fortunate to have more Easy Actions than Tough Actions to think about. Most of my patients seemed to have taken a general time-out and were just hunkering down and waiting for the storm to pass. But I knew that there were difficult days ahead for mental health professionals after the virus was defeated. This calamitous crisis would have lasting aftershocks for us all.

STEP 4: PULL BACK. Definitely one of the most important opportunities the crisis gave me was reflecting on my life and thinking how I could bring more quality into each activity, each contact, and each task on a daily basis. I thought about being more present in the moment when talking to my children and to my mother, when making food, writing reports, and even doing exercise. I have always been very active in sports and remember how the coaches used to say to do push-ups slowly and feel every muscle in your body when you do it. The yoga instructor at the gym would urge us to start the movement from our core, and then slowly outward. I remember hearing it, but not really understanding it other than superficially. It seemed a bit silly: why take time with one thing when you can do ten times the amount in the same amount of time? I guess it had never sunk in earlier, but now it made more sense to me. I wanted to bring that quality of focus to everything I did moving forward. I've been trying to practice this approach in my daily activities, and I feel it has certainly increased the quality of my life.

STEP 5: HOLD ON AND LET GO. Personality traits and characteristics are something I work with every day, but not since my psychology studies had I thought about it in terms of me. (It's always easier to describe and characterize others than yourself.) Now I forced myself to think through what traits and characteristics I thought were good for me to hold on to and cultivate and which ones to downplay moving forward.

I found that my silly and creative abilities made me happy and were valued by my friends and colleagues. Those were qualities that I would consciously put on a longer leash, while my more perfectionistic and self-critical tendencies would be given a much shorter leash. In fact, I would work to pack up these negative traits and "shelter" them in the basement along with all the other junk I have stored down there (just can't seem to find the time to throw it out, though); next to a box where I would pack away the need to control everything. Ironically, despite my isolation, practicing letting go of control and trusting more are the most important lessons I learned from working through the Five Steps during this challenging period.

Moving forward during the pandemic became as much a mental journey through my past as a journey into my future.

Like most of the world, I was at a crossroads where I could pivot in the direction of my choice. It was up to me. No matter what the current crisis brought in its wake, giving my best effort at making a brighter future for everyone I could touch was within my grasp—albeit, from an appropriate distance.

My COVID Crisis
Jennifer

Waking up to a global pandemic just weeks after turning in a manuscript for a book on solving life crisis was surreal. I wanted to jump online, start giving seminars, get the steps out there, but that just isn't possible in the publishing world. I was left having to be an "expert" on mental health with many of my tools (like these five steps) temporarily removed from my public toolbox.

The initial weeks were challenging—moving my practice home, transitioning to an entirely telemedicine practice, with limited IT support, an assistant far away, having to figure out prescriptions, the handling of handwritten therapy notes; basically, my day-to-day practice of medicine had to be reinvented overnight, without skipping a beat. It was a rough start.

As fate would have it, I was stuck alone during "shelter-in-place." I had to figure out life without the in-person support I've always known. As I prepared my taxes I learned someone had stolen my identity and filed taxes in my name, stealing my refund. As the crisis was growing, many of my patients were struggling, so my hours of patient care increased, and I was left trying to cram in calls to the IRS (voicemail) and to anyone who could tell me what to do about my tax situation. Of course, I also had the same issues we all had: the eeriness of getting groceries in a facemask, the lack of toilet paper, the online hysteria, the conspiracy theories that help no one and serve no purpose other than fostering anger and mistrust. We all experienced the same situation, but differently. Some of us were in high-impact areas, some were not. Some of us lost jobs, some did not. Some suffered alone, others suffered at the hands of those in their shared home. Some kept their health, some did not. We each have a story to tell.

As I'm writing this I'm still in isolation, still having to be flexible about the future. I'm still in it, so my steps are ongoing, and I change them as I go, as new needs and challenges emerge. I'm still a work in progress. But that's the point, isn't it? These life crises we face—cancer, loss, abuse, depression—are never magically solved one day by some declaration. We work through them, beyond them, and sometimes can't see around the corner where life's path is taking us. Here is how I'm using the five steps right now.

STEP ONE: GET A GRIP. Okay, you know the basics: cut off from in-person contact with family and friends, increased work hours (a blessing given how many people are out of work, but emotionally quite challenging given the patients I've known for years are suffering and in need of more intensive care), lots of after-hours emergency calls; loss of exercise routine, hugs, weekly brunches and walks with friends; the hours it takes for a simple grocery run, the anxiety of the unknown. Throw in my identity being stolen along with my tax refund, being separated from my mother who has significant health issues, and I think the surface of the problem is easily identified. But what does this mean to me?

I'm a happy introvert and find freedom in being alone (not *all* the time, but I probably enjoy it more than the average person), but in my worst moments the isolation struck a deep root. My shift in perception was a surprise to me. I was going through old travel photos and ran across a favorite—an old tunnel in a small ancient village in Tuscany. I have loved this photo all the years since I took it. I remember the feeling I had in the tunnel—wanting to stop and touch all the stones that were hundreds of years old, and at the same time wanting to run like a child to the end to see where it would lead me. This time, however, I was shocked to encounter a sense of darkness in the photo. Instead of feeling excited curiosity, I felt the tunnel leading towards some kind of impending doom. It hit me hard. Was my outlook changing?

I started having some really difficult days, feeling a vague sense of loss, loneliness. Part of this was the obvious—let's face it, a pandemic is a dark time, and I have many friends on the "front lines" putting their health and lives at risk to treat their patients. But part of this came from somewhere deeper.

When I was very young, my dad left the family. As an adult (and psychiatrist), I know this abandonment was his flaw, not mine. He was the one who should have been genetically programmed to take care of me and to support me, and he didn't. But children don't understand this, and internalize these things, and over the years loss has sometimes brought on the belief *I will always be alone, because no one wants me; no one will ever take care of me. I will always have to take care of myself alone.* It's a vulnerable admission to publish in a book—trust me—but I know I'm not the only one with these moments, feeling unworthy of love despite knowing I'm worthy of love. It's my own battle of emotion vs. logic, and to move forward from my sadness, I had to once again recognize and acknowledge its origins, as distant as they felt.

STEP TWO: PINPOINT WHAT YOU CAN CONTROL

What couldn't I control? I couldn't control whether I or someone I love got COVID. I couldn't control the pandemic, the length of "shelter-in-place" orders, the increase in psychiatric and addiction emergencies in my practice, the identity theft and tax fraud, and my unpredictable changes in mood.

What could I control? I could control my schedule and have some control over my social life, too. I could control whether I exercise, what I do with free time, how often I'm in communication with friends and loved ones, colleagues, neighbors, and how I interact with them.

What could I do about the things I couldn't control? I could work on staying in the present, not fantasizing about the myriad potential negative outcomes in the future—my investments, my financial security, my mother's health. I could work on my attitude, and focus on compassion and kindness. I could contact the IRS and the office of my local Congressional Representative to ask about federal and state tax fraud. I could call my CPA and attorney to find out the next steps (it's not like this hasn't happened to other people before, right?), and set up credit monitoring. To help with the changes in mood that occur every few days, I could open up. I could create a few texting groups— with coworkers, old friends, other psychiatrists. I could focus my emotions into writing blogs. If I know a certain time of day is typically rough, I could brainstorm options for facing it.

STEP THREE: PUSH INTO MOTION. I am motivated by necessity (I certainly don't want to lose my job), and my desire to feel as healthy as possible and as emotionally steady and happy as possible. I want to have full focus on my patients during their appointments, and I know the healthier I am, the greater my ability to hold their problems, their sorrows, their medical and emotional needs, and to walk with them through their stories. Like everyone, I have some tasks that are tougher than others, and starting with the easier ones gives me a sense that I'm getting *something* accomplished, even if it's just the dishes (seriously—there are so many more dishes!).

My Easy Actions: I needed a dedicated work space at home, and wanted it to be as peaceful and beautiful as possible, without spending money. I foraged in my back garden and in the empty lot on my street for wildflowers, and started making small arrangements for my table. When I was feeling overwhelmed, I'd run some laundry or load the dishwasher, just to give myself the sense that life was moving along "normally." I set time for what I call a "five-minute clean," when I straighten up as much as I can, but only have to spend five minutes doing it. It is literally amazing how much you can straighten up in only five minutes, and it makes a huge difference on the environment and my level of stress. Every evening I open the back doors for fresh air, to welcome the longer days, and started lighting candles every night for a relaxing glow. My mom and I text and talk all the time, but we started video calls. And don't laugh, but I have some squirrels in my yard, and they are so friendly that I decided to see whether I could train them. It sounds ridiculous, but I love animals and being able to watch them up close (not too close!) was an easy action that brought (still brings) a lot of joy.

My Tough Actions: It has been challenging to set new routines. My local market shortened its hours to literally my work hours, so I was left with weekends, and it was very crowded, and supplies were limited. I've had to be creative. I admittedly put off dealing with the tax fraud and identity theft (it's not like it wouldn't be waiting for me) to focus on stabilizing myself so I could better stabilize my patients. An acquaintance of mine started a fitness challenge on Facebook, so I jump-started a new exercise routine, which involved getting outdoors when possible, and finding online dance classes, yoga, and doing some Pilates and other cardio at home. I worked on acceptance. As a psychiatrist I know *all* the coping and relaxation tools and was using them, but was still having some ups and downs. I had to accept I am part of a community in an unprecedented crisis, and have to grieve like everyone else. I worked on changing my focus, and allowed myself to be vulnerable with colleagues and with friends. Two of my fellow psychiatrists and I put together a webinar for other mental health workers, opening the discussion of how we will need our own support moving forward, as the tsunami of anxiety, depression, and trauma flows toward us in the time ahead. I did finally get the required paperwork so I can file my taxes and get my refund. I will fill it all out when I've made my editor's deadline.

STEP FOUR: PULL BACK. I'll be honest, I'm a good reflector. I probably spend too much time thinking, and sometimes err on the side of overthinking, but my life is in a perpetual step four. It comes naturally. In crisis, it isn't as appealing.

I stopped watching local and cable news, and even got off social media for a while; the constant bombardment of the same news coming at me over and over really stressed me out. I check a single international news app on my phone, and I glance at the headlines twice daily. That's it for now. I just need to simplify the outside noise. I did make a secret Instagram account and only follow accounts that add joy to my life. I follow international designers, gardeners, florists, artists, baby goat pages, and people who make hand-painted wallpaper, French crystal, or who restore old châteaux in France. In short, this account is total eye candy. It offers brief escape, space to dream about my home, future travel. It has been a wonderful distraction from loneliness and stress.

I have been reflecting on how my relationships are changing, thinking about how I can have my emotional needs met in the current uncertain circumstances, and how I can meet my friends' needs, too. I'm thinking about my "hug crisis," my personal life, my personal and professional goals.

I have long understood the intimate connection between my brain and my environment. When I'm stressed, the space around me becomes more cluttered, and when my space is cluttered I feel more cluttered. I'm happiest when my home is clean and looks appealing. I started moving things around, regrouping candles and vases and even some furniture. Simple changes like creating a new color combination in my work space make a huge difference in how I feel.

I scrolled through pictures from my favorite parties—dinners, celebrations, a film screening, holidays—and focused on my home itself being the keeper of all of those memories, knowing one day this home will resume its purpose, and until then it can remind me of all the gatherings and laughter.

I've been practicing yoga online with my instructor, and deep into a challenging pose she said, "Close your eyes and see the darkness." I know what she meant—she was instructing us to shut out the outside world, not look around the room and think about the dust bunnies, the holes in socks, or what's next. I know physically we see darkness when we close our eyes, and in yoga it helps us focus our minds on our bodies and the current moment. But there's another meaning lurking in those words.

STEP FIVE: HOLD ON AND LET GO. In my ongoing process, I am working to hold on to compassion—not just for others, but for myself as well. I'm holding on to my love of laughter and humor. I'm holding on to gratefulness, and I'm working on ways to hold on to community. I am trying to cling to open-mindedness and flexibility, and let go of perfectionist tendencies.

I also am trying to let go of frustration, unhelpful thought patterns and loops (e.g., "All I need is a hug!"), predictions, certain expectations. I am letting go of my hatred of video-conferencing (why roll my eyes at something that's here to stay?), and, in a longer process, I am working on letting go of envy and fear of the unknown.

Acknowledgments

Jennifer

First, my mom—my rock, my support, my cheerleader, my dreamer. You are a source of such inspiration, love, forgiveness, integrity, strength. You have always been my favorite person, except for that one year in junior high. You raised me with a paucity of possessions, and an abundance of love, dry humor, and green shag carpeting. I love and value you beyond words.

Kjell Tore—I'm remembering our first conversation. Not when we met, but the first real one, when I heard your life story. I kind of thought you were insane and I was in awe hearing about a life so whimsically patched together. I'm so calculated; you are a free spirit. And I knew in that moment you would be a friend whose very way of living would challenge my neatly constructed existence. You haven't let me down. Our collaboration was a joy, and I will hold on to fond memories of writing trips to Norway, the tough work of creating and defining and communicating the steps, but I am letting go of Norwegian brown cheese and tubes of "kaviar." It's true: your ideas are as numerous and circuitous as the curls atop your head. It drives me crazy while teaching me to step back from my sometimes myopic viewpoint to consider a new way of thinking. Your family and friends are welcoming and wonderful, and I thank you all.

Thank you, Greg Johnson, for agreeing to represent me, and for so much more. You are a coach and encourager, and bullishly pushed me into this topic even when I didn't see it. You knew. And you were right.

Thank you, Denise Silvestro, for agreeing to work with co-authors who each wanted (insisted) to use a unique voice. Your editing eye is gold, even from New York amid a pandemic. I'm speechless and love working with you.

To the Kensington team, all in New York, pressing on during unprecedented circumstances, I am in awe of your dedication when there were so many other more important things to worry about. Lynn Cully (publisher), Ann Pryor (publicity and marketing), Arthur Maisel (production editor), Steven Zacharius (Kensington CEO, a.k.a. the boss), and Shannon Plackis (my editor Denise's assistant). I want to fly to New York and hug each of you. (Not in a weird way.)

Thank you, Daniel Amen. You have seen and called out my potential from the beginning, when you heard me give a lecture on opioid dependence and offered me a job. You even encouraged me to do a PBS special! That's still not on this introvert's list, but I did finally find my courage to start making my voice heard. You have taught me how to push myself in new directions and fight for what I want. You've introduced me to some of the best physicians I have ever had the pleasure of working with and lent me your platform.

Thanks to my lifelong bestie, Charlotte Jensen, a talented writer and editor, who has probably been wondering how on earth I got a book deal but supported me nonetheless. My list of why I love you is long, but here I will thank you for teaching me how hard writing is for everyone (or at least pretending it is), for encouraging me to chill out, for sending memes and baby farm animal videos. Thank you for long-distance wine (whine?) dates and for being the friend who made an "album" with me during that short-lived yet apparently inspiring Dead Milkmen phase we went through.

Thank you to my friends. My greatest talent is being a collector of good people. (And candlesticks.) I have friends from age four, every stage of education and training, all the places I've lived, the "randoms" I've met along the way on airplanes, through social media, at Bloomingdale's, and through networking or a night out on the town. Thank you for giving me ab-workout laughter, hugs, tears, life. You are as close to the feeling of a Hallmark Christmas movie I'll ever have (with the exception of Lillehammer in December, obviously). We've walked through our share of joys as well as crises together—divorces, financial ruin, health scares, surgeries, losses, births, late-night studying, maybe a party or two, a board exam involving a high-rise fire and evacuation, and one involving a tornado, and seventeen seasons of *Top Chef*. I seriously love each one of you.

Everyone here contributed in some way to the courage it took for me to take a hammer to the glass box I've kept myself in. Thank you.

Kjell Tore

Writing a book about life crises involves reflecting over your own life crises. The key question in the face of adversity is: Are you alone or do you have a team behind you? I want to thank the people who have been with me through thick and thin. My mother, Anne-Lise, and my children, Lars Henrik, Frida Sofie, and Benjamin, my bonus kids, Malin, Marcus, Vilde, and Frida, and my brother and sister, Grant and Alissa. Without any of them, my team would have been a much weaker side. I also want to thank my father, Job Kjell, my aunts Inger, Tordis, Liv, and my uncles Herlof, Arne, and Svein, who with their personalities and character have given me as much inspiration as other giants in my life: Socrates, Kant, and Eglantyne Jebb.

An awesome group of talented individuals is behind this publication. My co-author Jennifer is as brilliant as she is genuine. Learning to know her and her way of breaking down complexity into its elementary parts has been a transformative experience for me (it might have to do with her chemistry background and/or her obsession with Norwegian chocolate). She has a tradition of choosing a word of the year, and my word of the year when working with her on the book was *Awake*. We have laughed and laughed through the process of writing this book. If Jennifer and I are the co-parents of this literary creation, our agent, Greg Johnson, is the "Godfather," who assigned us a mission to conceive. Our exceptional editor, Denise Silvestro, and the talented team at Kensington, including Steven Zacharius, Lynn Cully, Ann Pryor, Arthur Maisel, and Shannon Plackis, secured a safe and healthy delivery in the midst of a frightful pandemic, and Dr. Daniel Amen of Amen Clinics was the knight in shining armor.

My deepest respect and admiration goes to an incredible researcher who opened doors for me and supervised my dissertation in developmental neuropsychology, Professor Merete Glenne Øie, my brothers-in-arms during my doctorate Per Normann Andersen and Eric Winther Skogli, and other inspirational co-authors on peer-reviewed articles and book chapters: Elkhonon Goldberg, Kerstin Plessen, and Jens Egeland (all professors with caring, warm, and meticulous instincts). Without these individuals sharing with me their insights into the brain–behavior interface, I would not have been able to co-author this book. Their scientific rigor and integrity are models to emulate.

A heartfelt thanks to the many patients I have had the honor of getting to know over the course of my time as a clinician both in private practice and at various hospital posts. They have taught me with their lives as their canvas the importance of understanding everyone as a supremely precious individual with a unique combination of strengths and weaknesses—each and every one of us.

A special thanks to my boss (and psychiatric nurse) at Innlandet Hospital Trust, Marianne Fosstveit, and the many outstanding colleagues I work with, such as Kirsti Stavø (psychologist), Tor Anders Andersen (psychiatric nurse), and Sonja Vatn (psychiatrist), who always have time to listen with their hearts and provide golden nuggets of advice on difficult cases at work, on life, and/or on crazy book projects ("Well, you have to spend your spare time on something, don't you . . ."). And I bow deeply in gratitude to my test assistants Pia Johnsen and Hege Ragnhildsløkken, both outstanding occupational therapists helping me do my job.

My dear friend who introduced me to neuropsychology, Jan-Magne Krogstad, and Louise Angen Krogstad (yes, they are married) are the best friends anyone could ever have—btw, don't tell Louise that JM just bought expensive new speakers. Odd Inge has been my rock during some rocky years, and where would I be without friends such as Erland, Terje, Mari, and Unni. There is a long list of dear friends without borders who will remain unnamed here, just as kind and gentle forces in nature work their magic unseen, but without whom my world could not have moved forward.

I am blessed with an American family, a Lillehammer family, an Oslo family, a family of eminent colleagues, a nutty family of Pink Chicks, and an entire nation of "koselig" Viking trolls way up here in Northern Europe, who all stick together in times of need (with the exception of one or two outliers who keep the rest of us scrambling toward the centerline of our small boat to keep it stable). The strongest bonds are not always blood relations. We are all one family—and we are all together and united in this thing we call life.

Connect with 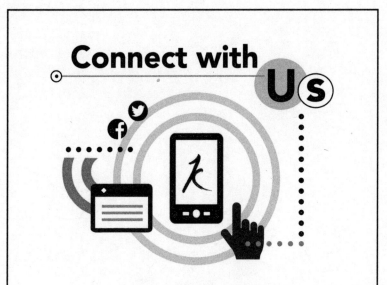U s

Visit us online at
KensingtonBooks.com
to read more from your favorite authors, see books
by series, view reading group guides, and more.

Join us on social media

for sneak peeks, chances to win books and prize packs,
and to share your thoughts with other readers.

facebook.com/kensingtonpublishing
twitter.com/kensingtonbooks

Tell us what you think!

To share your thoughts, submit a review,
or sign up for our eNewsletters, please visit:
KensingtonBooks.com/TellUs.